Current **CONTROVERSIES**

Assisted Suicide

Other Books in the Current Controversies Series

Alternative Therapies

Anger Management

Disaster Response

Family Violence

Homeland Security

Human Trafficking

Homeschooling

Media Ethics

The Rights of Animals

Smoking

Vaccines

Assisted Suicide

Sylvia Engdahl, Book Editor

GREENHAVEN PRESS
A part of Gale, Cengage Learning

Detroit • New York • San Francisco • New Haven, Conn • Waterville, Maine • London

Christine Nasso, *Publisher*
Elizabeth Des Chenes, *Managing Editor*

© 2009 Greenhaven Press, a part of Gale, Cengage Learning

Gale and Greenhaven Press are registered trademarks used herein under license.

For more information, contact:
Greenhaven Press
27500 Drake Rd.
Farmington Hills, MI 48331-3535
Or you can visit our Internet site at gale.cengage.com

For product information and technology assistance, contact us at

Gale Customer Support, 1-800-877-4253
For permission to use material from this text or product, submit all requests online at
www.cengage.com/permissions

Further permissions questions can be emailed to permissionrequest@cengage.com

Articles in Greenhaven Press anthologies are often edited for length to meet page requirements. In addition, original titles of these works are changed to clearly present the main thesis and to explicitly indicate the author's opinion. Every effort is made to ensure that Greenhaven Press accurately reflects the original intent of the authors. Every effort has been made to trace the owners of copyrighted material.

Cover photograph reproduced by permission of Alexander Gitlits, 2008. Used under license from Shutterstock.com.

LIBRARY OF CONGRESS CATALOGING-IN-PUBLICATION DATA

Assisted suicide / Sylvia Engdahl, book editor.
    p. cm. -- (Current controversies)
    Includes bibliographical references and index.
    ISBN-13: 978-0-7377-4132-2 (hardcover)
    ISBN-13: 978-0-7377-4133-9 (pbk.)
    1. Assisted suicide--Popular works. I. Engdahl, Sylvia.
    R726.A854 2009
    179.7--dc22

        2008023279

Printed in the United States of America
2 3 4 5 6   13 12 11 10 09

ED139

Contents

Foreword   13

Introduction   16

Chapter 1: Should Assisted Suicide Be Legalized?

Overview: Assisted Suicide Should Be   22
a Legal Right

Carl Wellman

It is cruel to require terminally ill patients to suffer untreatable pain or to lose their dignity; they should be allowed to end their lives.

Yes: A Right to Physician-Assisted Suicide Should Be Legally Recognized

Medically Hastened Deaths Already Occur   31
and Should Be Legal

Richard Ikeda

Terminally ill patients have a right to a dignified death, yet suicide attempts are often botched without a physician's aid. Physicians should legally be allowed to dispense life-ending drugs to terminally ill patients.

Individuals Should Have a Legal Right   35
to Choose Death

Thomas A. Bowden

People should not need the government's or anyone else's permission to die, and religious conservatives should not be allowed to force their views on others via the law.

Assisted Suicide Is a Pressing Social Need   38
and Should Be Legalized

Uwe-Christian Arnold, interviewed by
Julie Gregson

Some governments want to avoid dealing with the issue of assisted suicide, but the legal availability of assisted suicide is needed in today's society.

No: Legalizing Assisted Suicide Would Harm Society

Legalizing Assisted Suicide Would Put People
Without Health Insurance at Risk

Robert P. Jones, interviewed by David Masci

The debate over assisted suicide is not a battle between conservatives and liberals. Many political liberals oppose legalization because inequities in America's health-care system makes it impossible to implement in a way that will not endanger disadvantaged citizens.

44

Legalizing Assisted Suicide Would Devalue
the Lives of the Disabled and Severely Ill

Teresa Favuzzi

Making assisted suicide legal would create pressure to opt for it on the basis of keeping health-care costs down and would foster the belief that some lives are not worth living.

53

Legalizing Assisted Suicide Would
Undermine Patients' Trust in Physicians

American Geriatrics Society

Physicians should alleviate suffering, not intentionally terminate life. Allowing them to assist in suicide would harmful to vulnerable members of society.

56

Legalized Assisted Suicide Reflects a Biased
View of the Disabled

Samuel R. Bagenstos

Disability rights activists oppose legalizing assisted suicide because it encourages the idea that disability leads to despair and because they do not believe any safeguards could protect the disabled from being coerced into choosing suicide.

60

Chapter 2: Is Assisted Suicide Moral?

Chapter Preface   65

Yes: Assisted Suicide Is Compatible with Moral Principles

Religious Objections to Assisted Suicide   67
Contradict the Premise of Free Will

Alvaro Vargas Llosa

Although most religious groups oppose assisted suicide, their argument against it is not consistent with their belief in free will or with their conviction that the soul outlives the body.

Religious and Spiritual Principles Lead   70
to Support of Assisted Suicide

Kenneth W. Phifer

Mere existence is not the highest value and suffering has no inherent moral worth. Society does not have the right to disregard individual autonomy and force people to go on living in spite of pain that can never be relieved.

A Just Reorganization of World Health-Care   79
Resources Could Lead to a Duty to Die

Margaret Pabst Battin

Several bioethicists have argued that terminally ill or elderly people have a duty to die in order to reduce the burden on others. If a way is found to distribute health-care resources equally throughout the world, this argument may become more valid.

No: Assisted Suicide Conflicts with Many People's Moral Convictions

Assisted Suicide Violates Christian Beliefs   91
About Human Life

Albert Mohler

Christians who advocate assisted suicide are not in accord with the teachings of Christianity about human life and death. Their views disregard Christianity's moral tradition.

The Wish to Die Is Based on Social as Well   **97**
as Medical Issues

Adrienne Asch

Most of the people who have chosen to die under
Oregon's assisted suicide law have done so not to relieve
their pain but because of social issues, such as loss of autonomy and dignity. A wish to die may be simply a response to the fear of being disliked or resented by potential caregivers.

Legalized Physician-Assisted Suicide   **104**
Empowers Doctors, Not Patients

Sheldon Richman

Physician-assisted suicide laws do not provide patient autonomy, as the patient must petition a doctor for permission to die. This is wrong because suicide is a moral issue rather than a medical one and a doctor's judgment
should not prevail over a person's free choice.

Chapter 3: Would Assisted Suicide Be a Slippery Slope?

Chapter Preface   **108**

Yes: Legalizing Assisted Suicide Would Encourage Hastened Death

Assisted Suicide Will Not Remain Restricted   **110**
to the Terminally Ill

Wesley J. Smith

Advocates of assisted suicide have insisted that it would
be available only to the terminally ill, but now some are
arguing that anyone who is suffering, including the mentally ill, should be eligible.

Legalized Assisted Suicide May Lead to   **115**
Legalized Euthanasia

Susan W. Enouen

Data on assisted suicide in Oregon suggest that not all of
the law's original safeguards are being observed and that
public acceptance is increasing. Experience in the Netherlands has shown that such acceptance can lead to legalization of euthanasia.

Use of Euphemisms Attempts to Ease   **120**
Acceptance of Assisted Suicide

Rita L. Marker and Wesley J. Smith

Advocates now object to the term "assisted suicide" and
for political reasons prefer "assisted death" or "aid in dying." The government of Oregon no longer uses the word
"suicide," but the press so far has not acquiesced.

Research That Found No Slippery Slope   **126**
Effect Was Invalid

Meg Jalsevac

A study asserting that legalization of assisted suicide in
Oregon and in the Netherlands did not result in an increase in deaths of vulnerable people has been strongly
criticized on the grounds that the research methods employed were not valid.

**No: Legalizing Assisted Suicide Would Not
Lead to More Deaths**

Legalized Assisted Suicide Does Not Lead to   **130**
Increased Suicide Among the Disadvantaged

University of Utah

A recent study conducted by the University of Utah found
that deaths among vulnerable people did not increase after legalization of assisted suicide in Oregon and in the
Netherlands, except in the case of AIDS patients.

Legalizing Assisted Suicide Prevents Harm   **135**
to the Vulnerable

Peter Singer

The slippery slope debate used to be speculative, but now
there is evidence from Oregon and several countries that
assisted-suicide laws are not being abused. On the contrary, such laws bring the issue into the open where it
can be scrutinized.

Chapter 4: Does Assisted Suicide Work Well Where It Is Practiced?

Overview: Legalized Assisted Suicide
in Oregon   143

Colin Fogarty

Supporters of Oregon's Death with Dignity law believe that it has proven successful, and even its opponents recognize that it is unlikely to be changed.

Yes: Legalized Physician-Assisted Suicide Is Helping the Terminally Ill

Legalized Physician-Assisted Suicide Results
in Peaceful Death   146

Don Colburn

A woman who chose physician-assisted suicide in Oregon had a party for friends and family on the day she took a lethal drug, and then died peacefully according to her plan.

People Consider Assisted Suicide for Both
Physical and Psychological Reasons   154

*Dean Blevins, Thomas A. Preston, and
James L. Werth Jr.*

A study of healthy people who favor physician-assisted suicide shows that their attitudes match those of people who have employed the law in Oregon.

Europeans Increasingly Support
Assisted Suicide   163

Donna Casey

Many people from countries where assisted suicide is illegal travel to Switzerland, where the practice is legal. In The Netherlands, even active euthanasia is legal, but is subject to strict controls.

No: Assisted Suicide Is Causing Many Kinds of Problems

Official Data on Assisted Suicide in Oregon
Are Unreliable   168

Rita L. Marker

Official data about physician-assisted suicide in Oregon
may not be reliable because it comes from the doctors
involved, who would not report their own failures to ob-
serve the rules. As such, the law offers more protections
to doctors than to patients.

Doctors Are Negatively Affected by Assisting
in Suicide   179

Kenneth R. Stevens Jr.

Doctors do not like assisting in suicide and many of
them suffer emotional and psychological effects from the
procedure, or from feeling pressured by patients to provide such assistance.

Volunteers Are Assisting in Suicides Where
It Is Not Legal   189

Paul Rubin

Assisted-suicide advocates help people die in states where
physician assistance is not legal. Usually they are not
prosecuted as long as patients procure their own means
of ending their lives, but some volunteers risk being
charged with manslaughter.

Assisted Suicides in Public Places Spur
Protests in Switzerland   199

DPA News

The Swiss organization Dignitas, which legally assists suicides of foreign tourists, is facing opposition in neighborhoods where public suicides and the frequent presence of hearses have become objectionable.

Organizations to Contact   202

Bibliography   210

Index   218

Foreword

By definition, controversies are "discussions of questions in which opposing opinions clash" (Webster's Twentieth Century Dictionary Unabridged). Few would deny that controversies are a pervasive part of the human condition and exist on virtually every level of human enterprise. Controversies transpire between individuals and among groups, within nations and between nations. Controversies supply the grist necessary for progress by providing challenges and challengers to the status quo. They also create atmospheres where strife and warfare can flourish. A world without controversies would be a peaceful world; but it also would be, by and large, static and prosaic.

The Series' Purpose

The purpose of the Current Controversies series is to explore many of the social, political, and economic controversies dominating the national and international scenes today. Titles selected for inclusion in the series are highly focused and specific. For example, from the larger category of criminal justice, Current Controversies deals with specific topics such as police brutality, gun control, white collar crime, and others. The debates in Current Controversies also are presented in a useful, timeless fashion. Articles and book excerpts included in each title are selected if they contribute valuable, long-range ideas to the overall debate. And wherever possible, current information is enhanced with historical documents and other relevant materials. Thus, while individual titles are current in focus, every effort is made to ensure that they will not become quickly outdated. Books in the Current Controversies series will remain important resources for librarians, teachers, and students for many years.

In addition to keeping the titles focused and specific, great care is taken in the editorial format of each book in the series. Book introductions and chapter prefaces are offered to provide background material for readers. Chapters are organized around several key questions that are answered with diverse opinions representing all points on the political spectrum. Materials in each chapter include opinions in which authors clearly disagree as well as alternative opinions in which authors may agree on a broader issue but disagree on the possible solutions. In this way, the content of each volume in Current Controversies mirrors the mosaic of opinions encountered in society. Readers will quickly realize that there are many viable answers to these complex issues. By questioning each author's conclusions, students and casual readers can begin to develop the critical thinking skills so important to evaluating opinionated material.

Current Controversies is also ideal for controlled research. Each anthology in the series is composed of primary sources taken from a wide gamut of informational categories including periodicals, newspapers, books, U.S. and foreign government documents, and the publications of private and public organizations. Readers will find factual support for reports, debates, and research papers covering all areas of important issues. In addition, an annotated table of contents, an index, a book and periodical bibliography, and a list of organizations to contact are included in each book to expedite further research.

Perhaps more than ever before in history, people are confronted with diverse and contradictory information. During the Persian Gulf War, for example, the public was not only treated to minute-to-minute coverage of the war, it was also inundated with critiques of the coverage and countless analyses of the factors motivating U.S. involvement. Being able to sort through the plethora of opinions accompanying today's major issues, and to draw one's own conclusions, can be a complicated and frustrating struggle. It is the editors' hope that Current Controversies will help readers with this struggle.

Introduction

"The law has always recognized a distinction between letting a patient die and making that patient die. The Supreme Court concluded [that state bans against physician-assisted suicide do not violate the U.S. Constitution.]"

Physician-assisted suicide (PAS) has become increasingly controversial over the past two decades. Only one state, Oregon, has legalized the practice, despite hard-fought campaigns in several other states to legalize it as well. To fully comprehend the controversy, it is important to understand what the term "assisted suicide" means in the context of these debates. In the first place, it always refers to assistance by a doctor, even when the word "physician" is omitted; no state has ever considered allowing anyone other than a physician to aid in a suicide, and in most states being an accomplice in a suicide is explicitly defined as a crime. In the second place, "assistance" means prescribing lethal drugs that a gravely ill patient may choose to take. It does not mean the actual injection of such drugs by the doctor, which is not assisted suicide but euthanasia, or mercy killing—something that is illegal everywhere in the United States. Nor does "assistance" mean simply discontinuing life-sustaining treatment at a patient's request. Patients have a legal right to refuse unwanted medical treatment, which is something quite different from suicide.

Recently, supporters of physician-assisted suicide have made an effort to distinguish this term from suicide as the word is used in other contexts. They have convinced some organizations, including the government of Oregon, to substitute terms such as "assisted death," "aid in dying," or "death with dignity" in its place. However, opponents believe that "suicide" is an accurate description, and neutral parties, including the media, continue to use it.

The U.S. Supreme Court has considered the issue of physician-assisted suicide in three separate cases. In two of them—*Washington v. Glucksberg* and *Vacco v. Quill*, both decided in 1997—the Court ruled unanimously that laws prohibiting PAS are not unconstitutional, thereby allowing individual states to determine its legality. In the third case—*Gonzales v. Oregon* (2006)—by a 6–3 decision the Court ruled that the government could not use the Controlled Substances Act to prevent doctors from prescribing lethal drugs under the provisions of Oregon's Death with Dignity law. All three of these cases aroused a great deal of media interest and public debate on a wide range of issues associated with allowing the terminally ill to request physicians' aid in dying. Even in the two unanimously decided cases, several of the justices wrote separate opinions expressing different views of the legal issues.

In the *Glucksberg* case, Dr. Harold Glucksberg, along with three other physicians, several patients, and the organization Compassion in Dying, argued that Washington State's ban on assisted suicide violated the Due Process Clause of the Fourteenth Amendment to the Constitution. They maintained that the personal liberties protected by that clause include the liberty to control the time and manner of one's death. The Court of Appeals agreed with them. Chief Justice William Rehnquist's Supreme Court majority opinion, however, stated that only liberties deeply rooted in the nation's history and traditions are protected, and—in contrast to the right to refuse unwanted medical treatment—no "right to die" has existed in the past. Although the Constitution also requires that legal prohibitions be related to legitimate government interests, the government certainly has an interest in the preservation of human life, said Chief Justice Rehnquist. Among other considerations, it has an interest in protecting vulnerable groups—including the poor, the elderly, and disabled persons—from abuse, neglect, and mistakes. The Court of Appeals dismissed the State's concern that disadvantaged persons might be pressured into physician assisted suicide as "ludicrous on its face." We have recognized, however, the real risk of subtle coercion and undue influence in end of life situations. . . . If physician assisted suicide were permitted, many might resort to it to spare their families the substantial financial burden of end of life health care costs.

Therefore, according to the Supreme Court, choosing to hasten death is not a fundamental liberty, nor is liberty the only factor to be considered when laws regarding physician-assisted suicide are passed. The Court held that Washington state's prohibition against causing and aiding in suicide does not violate the Due Process Clause of the U.S. Constitution.

Vacco v. Quill was decided by the Supreme Court on the same day as *Glucksberg*. In this case, a group of physicians contested New York State's law against physician-assisted suicide under a different clause of the Fourteenth Amendment, the Equal Protection Clause. The physicians argued that there is no difference between discontinuing lifesaving medical treatment and taking life-ending medication, since death is the result of both; and that it therefore constitutes inequality to allow some patients to hasten death by refusing treatment, yet prohibit others from hastening it by requesting a lethal prescription. Although the Court of Appeals had accepted this argument, the Supreme Court strongly disagreed, offering many reasons why the two are indeed different. First, there is the matter of intent. A patient who asks that treatment be discontinued may merely want to end uncomfortable procedures that will be of no benefit, and the physician may intend only to respect the patient's wishes, without aiming to cause death. When lethal medication is prescribed, however, the doctor plays a pivotal role in ending the patient's life. The law has always recognized a distinction between "letting a patient die and making that patient die." The Supreme Court concluded that the state of New York's ban on assisted suicide does not violate the Equal Protection Clause.

In *Gonzales v. Oregon*, the Supreme Court was divided. Alberto Gonzales at the time was U.S. attorney general, whose job it is to see that federal laws are enforced. In his opinion— and that of his predecessor John Ashcroft—assisted suicide was not a legitimate medical practice, even though it was legal in Oregon. John Ashcroft had declared that under the Controlled Substances Act (CSA)—the same law that applies to illegal drug dealers—physicians could not prescribe federally controlled drugs for the purpose of ending patients' lives, and if they did, they would lose their licenses to prescribe controlled substances for any purpose. The State of Oregon, joined by a physician, a pharmacist, and some terminally ill patients, had filed a lawsuit to prevent this from happening, and the lower courts had ruled in their favor. When the Supreme Court reviewed the case, the arguments presented on both sides dealt extensively with the pros and cons of assisted suicide. The Court's decision, however, was based on legal technicalities rather than on the question of whether assisted suicide is legal, despite media headlines that proclaimed "Supreme Court Upholds Oregon's Assisted Suicide Law," and the like. The majority held that the wording of the CSA is clearly intended to apply only to illegal drugs, not those that can be used for medicinal purposes, such as the relief of pain, and that it does not give the federal government the authority to override state laws concerning medical practice. In a dissenting opinion Justice Antonin Scalia wrote, "If the term '*legitimate* medical purpose' has any meaning, it surely excludes the prescription of drugs to produce death," but that issue was not the one on which the outcome hinged.

None of these Supreme Court decisions have bearing on whether or not physician-assisted suicide will be legalized by more states. "Throughout the Nation," wrote Rehnquist in *Washington v. Glucksberg,* "Americans are engaged in an earnest and profound debate about the morality, legality, and practicality of physician assisted suicide. Our holding permits this debate to continue, as it should in a democratic society."

CHAPTER 1

Should Assisted Suicide Be Legalized?

Overview: Assisted Suicide Should Be a Legal Right

Carl Wellman

Carl Wellman is emeritus professor of philosophy at Washington University in St. Louis and the author of several books.

Ought there to be a right to physician-assisted suicide under United States law? In this article I shall argue in the affirmative. I suggest that it should have the same basic structure as the various rights to physician-assisted suicide, constitutional or statutory, that have been claimed in federal and state courts during the past few years. It should be a rights-package, not a single complex right but a set of rights concerning distinct aspects of physician-assisted suicide. Specifically, it should consist of the bilateral liberty-rights to request or not request, to obtain or not obtain, and to use or not use assistance provided by one's physician to commit suicide. . . .

Who Would Have This Right?

Let me describe briefly the kind of legal right to physician-assisted suicide that I will defend. First, who would be the right-holders? The right would be possessed by all and only those patients who are either enduring intolerable unrelievable suffering or who are terminally ill. Many would limit the possession of the right to patients who are both terminally ill and enduring intolerable, unrelievable suffering, but to my mind this is too restrictive. I can see no convincing reason why those who are not terminally ill should be required by the law to endure extreme suffering for an even more extended period than those who will soon be released by death or what value would be protected by denying terminally ill

Carl Wellman, "A Legal Right to Physician-Assisted Suicide Defended," *Social Theory and Practice*, vol. 29, January 2003, pp. 19–38. Copyright © 2003 by *Social Theory and Practice*. Reproduced by permission of the publisher and the author.

patients the choice of hastening an inevitable death? Again, many would limit possession to those who are enduring suffering resulting from a bodily illness, but why deny relief to those, if any, who are enduring intolerable unrelievable suffering resulting from mental causes? I would agree, however, that even intolerable suffering should not qualify one for a legal right to physician-assisted suicide if the suffering can be rendered tolerable by medical management or eliminated by curing or arresting the illness from which it results. . . .

The law ought to promote the well-being of the citizens when it can do so effectively and without serious social costs.

The standard arguments in favor of a legal right to physician-assisted suicide are hardly news. It is frequently asserted that there ought to be a right to physician-assisted suicide under United States law in order to enable qualified patients to avoid unnecessary suffering, to enable qualified patients to die with dignity, and to respect those patients' right to autonomy or self-determination. Although I believe that these three arguments point in the right directions, they stand in need of a more precise formulation and fundamental justification than is usual. For one thing, it is essential to distinguish between reasoning from authoritative legal sources to conclusions about what the law is and reasoning from moral premises to what the law ought to be. "The Philosophers' Brief" [an amicus curiae, or friend of the court, brief presented to the U.S. Supreme Court in 1997 regarding the views of six philosophers on the topic of whether dying patients have the right to choose death] purports to consist of purely legal reasoning. "These cases do not invite or require the Court to make moral, ethical, or religious judgments about how people should approach or confront their death or about when it is ethically appropriate to hasten one's own death or

23

ask others for help in doing so." But in his introduction to it, Ronald Dworkin explains that its reasoning is both moral and legal. "First, it defines a very general moral and constitutional principle—that every competent person has the right to make momentous personal decisions which invoke fundamental religious or philosophical convictions about life's value for himself." Moreover, one should distinguish carefully between the principles of individual morality and the moral principles concerning public morality and legal institutions. Finally, those who have advanced these standard arguments have done far too little to justify the moral principles to which they appeal. Let us, therefore, re-examine each of these three arguments.

Someone who is enduring intolerable suffering ought to be free to end her life before her human capacities are irreparably damaged.

First, there ought to be a legal right to physician-assisted suicide in order to enable qualified patients to avoid unnecessary suffering. Some patients enduring intolerable, unrelievable suffering as well as some terminally ill patients who are enduring lesser but still severe suffering need this legal right, for they cannot escape from their suffering without it. Those who will die within hours or a very few days will soon obtain relief without taking any action, and those who are on life-prolonging intensive care can often end their lives simply by refusing continued treatment. But others are condemned to continuing severe suffering by any legal system that confers no legal right to physician-assisted suicide. To be sure, a few might be able to commit suicide without assistance and a few others might be able to find persons willing to violate the law in order to rescue them from their distress. But most patients would be unwilling to commit suicide under those conditions, for attempts to commit suicide often fail, leaving one in an even worse condition than before, and obtaining or using assistance from another to commit suicide could expose that person to legal sanctions.

The law ought to promote the well-being of the citizens when it can do so effectively and without serious social costs, and above all ought not to harm those subject to it unless this is necessary to prevent even greater harms. Any law that forces patients to endure avoidable suffering harms those patients, and any legal right that enables them to escape from suffering is, other things being equal, in the patients' best interests. A legal right to physician-assisted suicide creates an exception to those laws that otherwise would prevent or hinder qualified patients from escaping from severe suffering. Its core liberties would permit qualified patients to commit suicide with the assistance of their physicians, and its associated elements would go a long way toward enabling them to exercise the liberties to request, obtain, and use medical assistance from their physicians if, but only if, they choose to do so. Therefore, there ought to be a legal right to physician-assisted suicide unless such a right would bring with it very serious social costs or great harms.

Enabling Patients to Die with Dignity

Second, there ought to be a legal right to physician-assisted suicide to enable qualified patients to die with dignity. The concept of death with dignity is as profoundly important as it is obscure. The *Oxford English Dictionary* defines dignity as "the quality of being worthy or honourable" and reminds us that historically it has been persons of high estate or social rank who have been thought to be honorable. But [philosopher] Immanuel Kant maintained that there is something in human nature, irrespective of social status, that commands our respect. He believed that this is moral agency and that it confers dignity or inherent worth upon all human beings. Some such thought lies behind the demand for death with dignity.

Human beings share with many nonhuman animals the capacity to feel bodily pleasure and pain, perhaps even to experience happiness and to suffer mental distress. This calls for our concern and compassion. I agree with Kant that there is also something in normal human beings that commands our respect and constitutes an essentially human dignity. Although it consists primarily in our practical rationality and capacity for moral choice and action, as Kant held, I believe that it also includes other human capacities such as our imagination, creativity, the ability to communicate and interact with others, and sympathy or an awareness of and concern for the well-being or adversity of others. If this is so, then one's death lacks dignity when the process of dying has destroyed or degraded those essentially human capacities that command our respect. And death can be an indignity when the process of dying flagrantly reveals the gross deterioration of the capacities, such as self-control or the ability to interact meaningfully with others, that constitute one's dignity.

Why does it matter whether or not one dies with dignity? It is important to the patient because when and how one dies profoundly affects the meaning of one's death and, thus, the shape and significance of one's life. One's life is a biography experienced as a drama with a beginning, a middle, and an end such that the intrinsic value of each part is determined much more by one's awareness of its significance for the whole than by its felt pleasantness or painfulness. The awareness that one will die without dignity can undermine one's self-respect and cause one to devalue one's life. The loss of a patient's dignity also affects how others remember her and reduces, at least to some degree, their respect for her. This is an injury to the patient, who must now expect to be remembered less fondly and with less respect than she would wish, and a misfortune to friends and family members, who are condemned to live on with distressful memories of the death of their loved one.

The law ought not to harm patients and those who love them by denying qualified patients the opportunity to die with dignity. Someone who is terminally ill ought not to be forced to submit passively to a death beyond her control, but ought to be able to exercise her moral agency by deciding whether or not to end her life at a time and in a manner of her choosing. Similarly, someone who is enduring intolerable suffering ought to be free to end her life before her human capacities are irreparably damaged either by her suffering or by the illness causing her to suffer. Therefore, there ought to be a legal right to physician-assisted suicide to enable these patients to die with dignity.

The Right to Autonomy

The third standard argument is that there ought to be a legal right to physician-assisted suicide in order to respect the qualified patient's moral right to autonomy or self-determination. Although I find this argument very plausible, I hesitate to accept it at face value. I have not been able to find in the literatures of moral philosophy or biomedical ethics any clear definition of the content of the alleged moral right to autonomy, much less any convincing explanation of its grounds. . . . Hence, I prefer to rest my case on two more simple considerations that might well underlie a right to autonomy, the moral duty not to intrude into the life of another and the moral duty to respect the rational agency of others. . . .

The law ought not to limit or deny individual liberty except when necessary to protect important state interests. Obviously any laws that prohibit or seriously hinder a patient from committing suicide with the assistance of her physician limit the liberty of the individual patient and her physician. It is hard to see what important state interest would make it necessary to deny individuals who are terminally ill or are enduring intolerable, unrelievable suffering liberty in this manner. Therefore, there very probably ought to be a legal right to physician-assisted suicide.

Thus an examination of the three standard arguments in favor of a legal right to physician-assisted suicide reveals four reasons for state legislatures to enact statutes that would confer this right upon patients who are terminally ill or enduring intolerable unrelievable suffering resulting from an incurable illness. The several states ought to introduce and maintain a legal right to physician-assisted suicide in order to enable qualified patients to avoid unnecessary suffering, to enable them to die with dignity, to avoid intruding into their lives, and to avoid denying or limiting individual liberty unnecessarily. . . .

Efforts to Relieve Suffering

[Opponents say that] enacting a legal right to physician-assisted suicide is undesirable because it would reduce the need to introduce better ways of caring for the dying and improved techniques for relieving the suffering of most patients. Granted that both are often inadequate today, considerable progress has been made recently in both respects. Many argue that a right to physician-assisted suicide would retard, perhaps reverse, this progress by reducing its urgency. Because terminally ill patients could exercise this right in order to avoid an undignified death, there would be less need to use scarce medical resources to maintain high-quality hospice care. And because patients enduring intolerable suffering would also have this option, there would be less need to provide more effective pain management or more adequate psychological support services in hospitals or nursing homes. Thus, the introduction of a legal right to physician-assisted suicide would result in premature or unnecessary death for patients who would be much better served by sustaining our progress in the introduction of preferable alternatives.

Once more I insist that it is cruel to deny physician-assisted suicide to those patients who are terminally ill or enduring intolerable suffering, be they many or few, and for whom adequate hospice care and the relief of their agony are not yet available. It is unjust to sacrifice them for the sake of future patients who would benefit by desirable improvements in medical practice. Moreover, our society has no need to choose between enacting a legal right to physician-assisted suicide and continuing the improvement in caring for the dying and relieving suffering. Both reforms, legal and medical, can and should be vigorously pursued. If as a consequence very few patients choose to exercise their right to physician-assisted suicide, so much the better.

I conclude that each of the several states ought to enact a right to physician-assisted suicide. It would be useful for the various state statutes to differ in details, especially regarding protective regulations, in order to obtain empirical evidence concerning the least dangerous and most beneficial formulation. Still, all of the rights conferred should have the same basic structure. They should be possessed by all and only those patients who are either enduring intolerable, unrelievable suffering or terminally ill. They should be rights-packages consisting of three liberty-rights—the rights to request or not request, to obtain or not obtain, and to use or not use assistance provided by one's physician to commit suicide. In addition to its defining core bilateral liberty, each of these rights must include associated elements that confer dominion, freedom, and control over this liberty upon the right-holder. Among these will be the legal liberty of the attending physician to provide, subject to protective regulations, requested medical assistance to her patient.

I do not take the arguments against enacting a legal right to physician-assisted suicide lightly. They are serious arguments, both because they concern important public interests and because there is not yet sufficient empirical evidence to predict reliably how much, if at all, any such right would damage those interests. Nevertheless, I have explained why I do not believe that they outweigh the reasons in favor of enacting a legal right to physician-assisted suicide. These are to enable qualified patients to avoid unnecessary suffering, to enable them to die with dignity, to avoid intruding into their lives, and to respect their rational agency. These compelling moral considerations cry out for the reform of United States law to make it less inhumane and more just.

Medically Hastened Deaths Already Occur and Should Be Legal

Richard Ikeda

Richard Ikeda is a doctor who cares for low-income elderly patients as medical director of Health For All community clinics in California.

When cure is no longer possible, the majority of Californians, and the majority of California physicians, want dying patients to have the right to make end-of-life choices in accord with their own values and beliefs. I am disappointed that my own professional organization, the California Medical Association (CMA), continues to oppose terminal patients' end-of-life choices. As a physician caring for the poor and vulnerable elderly, I can tell you cancer and other terminal patients need better end-of-life care and choices. This week [October 27, 2007,] completed ten years' experience with Oregon's death with dignity law, and all studies show end-of-life care has improved for all Oregonians.

The CMA leadership continues to ignore the evidence that patient choice helps all those facing the end of life. It's time for CMA to join other medical groups in changing its position on aid-in-dying. Peer-reviewed research from Oregon shows that after almost 10 years, there is no evidence of a slippery slope [a course of action that leads from one unintended result to another] or that vulnerable populations have been harmed. A study published last month [October 2007] in the *Journal of Medical Ethics* by five researchers who exhaustively examined the effects of aid in dying in Oregon and the Netherlands debunks opponents' arguments that legalized aid-in-dying harms disabled people and other at-risk groups. The researchers concluded that there was no evidence of harm to the elderly, the uninsured, the, poor, or the disabled. The most recent study found that no vulnerable populations have been harmed in any way from the Oregon law. Yet CMA ignores this evidence and continues to base its opposition to patient choice on a fear of a "slippery slope." But there is no slippery slope. CMA appears to be making policy based on conservative Christian doctrine instead of relying on peer-reviewed studies and the opinion of end-of-life experts.

Medically hastened deaths—which happen already— should be done in the best of circumstances under true safeguards instead of botched attempts and violent suicides we see now.

Physicians Favor Legalization

The CMA opposition ignores the views of most physicians. A national survey of 677 physicians and 1,057 members of the general public by HCD Research in October 2005 revealed that the majority of both groups believe that physicians should be permitted to dispense life-ending prescriptions to terminally ill patients who have made a rational decision to die due to unbearable suffering. The survey indicated that nearly two-thirds of physicians (62%) and the general public (64%) believes that physicians should be permitted to dispense life-ending prescriptions. The CMA policy contradicts that of the Academy of Hospice and Palliative Care Medicine (AAHPM), the organization that represents physicians on the front line of end-of-life care—[which] changed its position from opposition to "studied" neutrality: "Excellent medical care . . . can control most symptoms . . . near the end of life. On occasion, however, severe suffering persists; in such a circumstance a patient may ask his physician for assistance in ending his life by providing Physician-assisted Death (PAD)."

The American Medical Women's Association (AMWA) "supports the right of terminally ill patients to hasten what might otherwise be a protracted, undignified, or extremely painful death. AMWA believes the physician should have the right to engage in practice wherein they may provide a terminally ill patient with, but not administer, a lethal dose of medication and/or medical knowledge, so that the patient can, without further assistance, hasten his/her death. This practice is known as Aid in Dying."

In addition, the American Public Health Association has parted ways with the CMA on this issue, and urges health educators, policy-makers, journalists and health care providers to recognize that the choice of a mentally competent, terminally ill person to choose to self-administer medications to bring about a peaceful death is not "suicide," nor is the prescribing of such medication by a physician "assisted suicide."

The choice of whether to hasten death at the end of a terminal illness should belong to the patient. I have always been in favor of a patient's right to a dignified death. Medically hastened deaths—which happen already—should be done in the best of circumstances under true safeguards instead of botched attempts and violent suicides we see now. At a minimum, allowing the patient to control their own pain management allows for more comfort than a doctor can provide in some cases.

Control over a dying patient's death should belong to the patient, not the federal or state government. It is the patient who is suffering. It is at this time, as in other pivotal times in the lives of our patients, that physicians should feel safe in serving their patients, protected and free to discuss all medical options at the end of life. The more choices patients have, the better.

Caring for dying patients includes the sacred duty to listen to their fears, communicate their options, and honor their choices for end of life care. It's time for CMA to abandon its opposition to patients' end of life choices.

Individuals Should Have a Legal Right to Choose Death

Thomas A. Bowden

Thomas A. Bowden is a legal analyst at the Ayn Rand Institute.

This month [October 2007] marks the tenth anniversary of Oregon's pathbreaking assisted suicide law. But despite legislative proposals in California and elsewhere, Oregon remains the only state to have provided clear procedures by which doctors can help end their dying patients' pain and suffering while protecting themselves from criminal prosecution.

For a decade now, Oregon doctors have been permitted to prescribe a lethal dose of drugs to a mentally competent, terminally ill patient who makes written and oral requests, consults two physicians, and endures a mandatory waiting period. The patient's free choice is paramount throughout this process. Neither relatives nor doctors can apply on the patient's behalf, and the patient himself administers the lethal dose.

Elsewhere in America, however, the political influence of religious conservatism has thwarted passage of similar legislation, leaving terminal patients with nothing but a macabre menu of frightening, painful, and often violent end-of-life techniques universally regarded as too inhumane for use on sick dogs or mass murderers.

Society Should Permit Assisted Suicide

Consider Percy Bridgman, the Nobel Prize–winning physicist who, at 79, was entering the final stages of terminal cancer. Wracked with pain and bereft of hope, he got a gun and somehow found courage to pull the trigger, knowing he was condemning others to the agony of discovering his bloody re-

Thomas A. Bowden, "After Ten Years, States Still Resist Assisted Suicide," Ayn Rand Institute, October 30, 2007. Copyright © 2007 Ayn Rand® Institute. (ARI) All rights reserved. Reproduced by permission.

mains. His final note said simply: "It is not decent for society to make a man do this to himself. Probably this is the last day I will be able to do it myself."

What lawmakers must grasp is that there is no rational basis upon which the government can properly prevent any individual from choosing to end his own life. When religious conservatives enact laws to enforce the idea that their God abhors suicide, they threaten the central principle on which America was founded.

The Declaration of Independence proclaimed, for the first time in the history of nations, that each person exists as an end in himself. This basic truth—which finds political expression in the right to life, liberty, and the pursuit of happiness—means, in practical terms, that you need no one's permission to live, and that no one may forcibly obstruct your efforts to achieve your own personal happiness.

But what if happiness becomes impossible to attain? What if a dread disease, or some other calamity, drains all joy from life, leaving only misery and suffering? The right to life includes and implies the right to commit suicide. To hold otherwise—to declare that society must give you permission to kill yourself—is to contradict the right to life at its root. If you have a duty to go on living, despite your better judgment, then your life does not belong to you, and you exist by permission, not by right.

The Right to Life Implies the Right to Death

For these reasons, each individual has the right to decide the hour of his death and to implement that solemn decision as best he can. The choice is his because the life is his. And if a doctor is willing (not forced) to assist in the suicide, based on an objective assessment of his patient's mental and physical state, the law should not stand in his way.

Religious conservatives' opposition to the Oregon approach stems from the belief that human life is a gift from the Lord, who puts us here on earth to carry out His will. Thus, the very idea of suicide is anathema, because one who "plays God" by causing his own death, or assisting in the death of another, insults his Maker and invites eternal damnation, not to mention divine retribution against the decadent society that permits such sinful behavior.

If a religious conservative contracts a terminal disease, he has a legal right to regard his own God's will as paramount, and to instruct his doctor to stand by and let him suffer, just as long as his body and mind can endure the agony, until the last bitter paroxysm carries him to the grave. But conservatives have no right to force such mindless, medieval misery upon doctors and patients who refuse to regard their precious lives as playthings of a cruel God.

Rational state legislators should regard the Oregon law's anniversary as a stinging reminder that 49 of the 50 states have failed to take meaningful steps toward recognizing and protecting an individual's unconditional right to commit suicide.

Assisted Suicide Is a Pressing Social Need and Should Be Legalized

Uwe-Christian Arnold, interviewed by Julie Gregson

Uwe-Christian Arnold is a German physician and the deputy director of Dignitate, the German branch of Dignitas, a Swiss organization that facilitates assisted suicides. Julie Gregson is a reporter for Deutsche Welle, Germany's international broadcaster.

The German branch of a Swiss right-to-die organization has unleashed a storm of protest by saying it is planning to carry out an assisted suicide in Germany. . . .

A few weeks ago [in November 2007] Dignitas hit the headlines for helping two Germans to die in a car park in Switzerland. The apparently undignified circumstances of their deaths sparked renewed criticism of the controversial organization, which has been accused of treating assisted suicide as a money-making enterprise.

While assisted suicide is legal in Switzerland, German law is much less clear-cut. Uwe-Christian Arnold, the deputy director of Dignitate, the German branch of Dignitas, and himself a doctor, says his group wants to set a legal precedent by carrying out an assisted suicide here in Germany. The head of the German doctors' chamber has called for Dignitate to be banned.

Julie Gregson: Why do you think your plan has created such an uproar in Germany?

Uwe-Christian Arnold: The reason that certain circles get so worked up about this topic is because it was completely taboo for decades. It was linked to euthanasia and the Nazis. Anyone who concerned themselves with this subject was lumped together with the Nazis. No one differentiated between the fact, for example, that no one asked the people who were killed then whether they wanted to die or not. Someone else decided that they should die. That is completely different from what we're planning.

The majority of people—82 percent of the Germans and the same numbers in England, in France, the US and Canada—are in favor of legalizing assisted suicide.

The precondition is that the patient wants to die and that they have legitimate reason to want to end their life. This is quite different from what the Nazis did. Doctors tend to be conservative and the German medical association is particularly conservative because it was closely involved with the Nazis. They have not dealt with this past over the last 60 years. On the occasions they did, it was always very uncomfortable. I don't want to reproach them for the fact that they want to avoid the topic of assisted suicide, but we have to deal with this topic. It is a pressing social need.

Have significant numbers of Germans been traveling to Switzerland to take up the services of Dignitas?

No, the numbers are not very significant. Last year [in 2006], there were 176 or so assisted suicides in total, 120 of those were Germans. That is a bit of an increase in the numbers of Germans, but it roughly corresponds to that of previous years. And it corresponds to the numbers going to other assisted suicide organizations, in Switzerland and in Oregon. The number of people who decide to end their lives in this way has remained steady.

Majority Favors Legalization

Why is assisted suicide such a pressing social need?

The majority of people—82 percent of the Germans and the same numbers in England, in France, the US and Canada—are in favor of legalizing assisted suicide. In Oregon it was made legal, but many other American [states] want it. And I think Germany should have it. It is a big country and the patients have big problems with this topic.

Is it partly a problem that was created by modern medicine?

It is exclusively a problem of medicine—high-tech medicine—that for decades has only been concerned with progress and it has notched up fantastic achievements. But it has completely forgotten that death also stands, lurks, at the end of all these strivings. Making this taboo can be very unpleasant for the patient. Many people have the experience that death can be dreadful with high-tech medicine. It can be something as simple as a feeding tube for an old person in a nursing-care home.

Every area in life is open to abuse. Abuse can always happen with or without assisted suicide.

Isn't it also partly a problem that the hospice system and palliative medicine isn't sufficient in Germany?

That is a very important factor. But even if we had such good palliative medicine and hospice provision as there is in Scandinavia—where they have provision for 20 percent of people against our 4 percent—then there would still be a very small minority who, if they got certain illnesses, would want to be able to determine the time when they die—and if they can with the help of a doctor. There are still illnesses that palliative medicine can't help, such as amyotrophic lateral sclerosis and multiple sclerosis.

There are certain preconditions that you have to fulfill to be eligible for assisted suicide. What are they?

You need to have a terminal illness or a serious illness that you can't live with anymore, one that handicaps you so strongly that you can no longer lead a dignified life. In other words, if you're lovelorn or you're suffering from an acute depression, then you won't be able to ask for assisted suicide.

Creating a Legal Precedent

Why are you trying to create a legal precedent here in Germany?

We are looking to set a test case because it is not clear whether a person can be prosecuted if they do not go to the aid of a person who is dying. There are judgments and a statement from the Ministry of Justice that confirms that you can do it under certain conditions, if the person has made the decision freely and that the will of the patient should be placed above the duty to preserve life.

Is it possible to protect this area from abuse?

In other countries, in the United States and, as far as I know, in the UK [United Kingdom], things are more advanced. There are ethical committees that meet and when there is an 86-year-old and he has a serious illness and he is due for a big operation, then they will discuss whether he should be operated on or given palliative medicine. A lot more is done to spare people from this hyper-medicine. That should be done more in Germany, too. It should be considered when there are cases where death might be the better solution. You don't have to kill them. You can just leave them. This can be entrusted in the hands of doctors. Of course, it is open to abuse. But this argument is not a good one. Every area in life is open to abuse. Abuse can always happen with or without assisted suicide.

You referred to ethical committees. Do you want to make assisted suicide into something that the state is involved in and remove it from the private sector?

That is the sense of our campaign that we get a sensible assisted-suicide policy in Germany. It shouldn't be the case that this only can be carried out in private. It should be possible in accordance with certain regulations as in Switzerland. In Switzerland, a doctor visits a patient after long and thorough preparation. You can't ring me and say, "Doctor, will you give me a lethal injection tomorrow?" That's out of the question. This topic is much too serious and much too sensitive for that.

The chief accusation that has been leveled at Dignitas is that it is trying to profit from people. And that Dignitas demands three times as much money as EXIT, another Swiss-based right-to-die group. What would you say to that?

EXIT has 50 million members and it carried out a constant number of assisted suicides a year, 35, 40 or 50 in a year. They have a certain price. For long-term members it is free and for those who have just recently joined, they take around 2,000 euros ($2,950). I can't tell you exactly, but they take a fee and it is lower than Dignitas. From their Swiss members Dignitas takes 2,000 euros. Only for those coming from abroad, they take more because they have cremation costs, counseling costs that are much higher than for people in Switzerland, who can just go to their local doctor. And then fees have to be paid to the Swiss authorities because costs are incurred by the foreigners. This isn't about making money. Dignitas has a large office and, unlike EXIT, which works with volunteers, it works consciously with professionals.

Do you think you will be successful with your demands?

Something will happen. There has been so much media attention. I think that if we make a test case, then we will see how they react. Only two things can happen. Either people will accept it, as with abortion in Germany. Or we will get a reactionary solution and fall back into the Middle Ages. But I'm hopeful. Because of the churches and the medical association, abortion was also completely taboo here for years, and nowadays we can perform abortion here just like in England and other countries.

Legalizing Assisted Suicide Would Put People Without Health Insurance at Risk

Robert P. Jones, interviewed by David Masci

Robert P. Jones is an independent consultant on religion and progressive politics and an affiliated scholar at the Center for American Progress. David Masci is a senior research fellow for the Pew Forum on Religion & Public Life.

The debate over physician-assisted suicide is often portrayed as a battle between social or religious conservatives who oppose the practice and liberals or progressives who support it. But not everyone fits neatly into this paradigm. For instance, Dr. Robert P. Jones, who calls himself a progressive, has just written a book urging liberal supporters of physician-assisted suicide (or physician aid in dying, as some supporters call it) to rethink their views, at least for now.

In *Liberalism's Troubled Search for Equality: Religion and Cultural Bias in the Oregon Physician-Assisted Suicide Debates,* published earlier this year [2007] by the University of Notre Dame Press, Jones argues that the debate over whether to allow physician aid in dying should wait until the United States guarantees adequate access to health care to all of its citizens. Jones, who does not in theory oppose physician-assisted suicide, argues that without health insurance terminally ill patients could end up choosing or be pressured into choosing to prematurely end their lives for financial or similar reasons. . . .

David Masci: You say in your book that both liberals and progressives incorrectly view physician-assisted suicide as another

Robert P. Jones, interviewed by David Masci, "A Progressive Argument Against the Legalization of Assisted Suicide," Pew Forum on Religion & Public Life, October 3, 2007. Copyright © 2008 Pew Research Center. Reprinted with the permission of the Pew Forum on Religion & Public Life, www.pewforum.org. Originally posted at http://pewforum.org/events/?EventID=157.

"choice" issue, like abortion. Why isn't this issue about someone's right to decide his or her fate at the end of life?

More vulnerable populations who are less likely to have health insurance and large financial resources are also less likely to support physician-assisted suicide.

Robert P. Jones: My argument is really a social-justice-oriented argument against the legalization of assisted suicide in our current health care context. And those last words are really important: in our current health care context. I think one important piece may be the number of uninsured Americans that we have in the country. The recent numbers that came out from the U.S. Census Bureau saw the number of Americans without health insurance rise to 15.8 percent—or 47 million people in our country. What that means—and what I argue—is that legalizing assisted suicide in the context where we have this kind of inequity in our health care system actually puts those who are uninsured at risk for reaching for assisted suicide for a financial necessity or out of some duress.

So to put it starkly, if you're faced with the choice at the end of life where one option is between $50 and $150 for a lethal prescription of medication to end your life versus tens of thousands or even hundreds of thousands of dollars for long-term care, that's a pretty draconian choice to put in front of people.

Low-Income People Opposed

You can see this situation coming out if you look at the demographics of people who are for and against assisted suicide. The country is fairly evenly divided if you look at Pew polling on this issue. But I argue that if you start looking underneath the numbers and you look at the poor or at minorities, a different picture emerges. According to my own analysis of the Pew data, you have 61 percent of whites with incomes over

$100,000 supporting physician-assisted suicide, but you have 78 percent of minorities with incomes under $50,000 opposing assisted suicide. That picture, I think, ought to tell us something—specifically, that those more vulnerable populations who are less likely to have health insurance and large financial resources are also less likely to support physician-assisted suicide. We shouldn't move too quickly past those numbers.

Arguments about the disadvantaged were dismissed because they were interpreted to be mere covers for the real agenda, which was a pro-life agenda.

A group that has been very prominent in these debates is the disability-rights movement. In August 2007 there was an article in the *Los Angeles Times* that cited opposition to assisted suicide coming from an unusual place—the disability-rights movement, which is concerned about people with disabilities being very vulnerable in our current health care context. That movement is really worried that financial incentives may push doctors to make certain decisions or push patients to make certain decisions that I think we couldn't call a free and non-coerced choice.

So what you are saying, in essence, is that lack of universal health care increases the risk that legalizing physician-assisted suicide will ultimately lead to abuses?

I think that's right. You mentioned earlier this analogy with abortion, that there's a kind of pro-life/pro-choice thing. I think one of the mistakes that has been made around the assisted suicide debate is to too easily try to fit that framework over this issue and say that if you're pro-life, you should be against physician-assisted suicide, and if you're pro-choice, you should be for it.

But I think that obscures the real financial issues here, and what I've been arguing is that a more appropriate analogy might be the capital punishment debate. That argument goes like this: Regardless of whether or not—in the abstract—we could justify capital punishment for certain heinous crimes, in the current context of our society, which is shot through with racism and shot through with financial problems of representation in the courts, we can't justly implement it.

And what I'm arguing is that a very similar kind of argument ought to be made by progressives on the issue of assisted suicide—that regardless of whether we can make an argument that physician-assisted suicide in certain cases is a social good or is morally justifiable, in our current health care context we can't justly implement it in a way that doesn't lead to increased risk to the disadvantaged and the vulnerable in society.

Let's assume that in the next few years the United States moves from its current health care system to a European-style universal care model and everyone has access to health care. That takes out of play your big concern. At that point, should people still have qualms about physician-assisted suicide? Are there still issues that need to be explored, or are we now ready to move on to that?

My argument is that [universal health care] ought to be the floor that is in place before we really have this debate. And at that point I think the argument is moving to a different space. I'm arguing that at least the justice claims of the poor, vulnerable and disabled ought to be met before we open up this debate, and I think it's a debate we ought to have. We ought to have it in the legislatures and in public, and it's one that I think is a healthy debate for the country.

One of the most interesting comments I found was by Dr. Rob Jonquiere, head of the Dutch Voluntary Euthanasia Society. He is a very strong advocate for these rights at the end of life in the context of the Netherlands, but when asked about what the U.S. ought to do, he basically said no. He said that in the U.S., where so many people are uninsured, you could not defend such a law. And this is from someone who is a staunch advocate for the right to assisted suicide and euthanasia at the end of life. And I think that really does set the floor below which we shouldn't go in the U.S.

Religious Opposition Often Misinterpreted

In your book you take liberals and progressives to task for ignoring the role that religion can play in this discussion. Why do you think the left has excluded religious considerations on an issue like doctor-assisted suicide?

Religious views got dismissed in the debate in a couple of ways that I find really unfortunate. The first one was by using language like, "You're imposing your religious beliefs on me on this issue." If you listen to the talking points of many of the supporters of Oregon's Death with Dignity Act and physician-assisted suicide, this is a tool that they reach for very quickly, this idea that any religious voice in the public debate is somehow imposing a view on someone else.

And that word "impose" carries a kind of sinister connotation, that there's something unconstitutional going on or there's something that we ought not to be doing. Famously, there was a commercial spot that ran in Oregon during these debates that painted a kind of sinister view of religious dogma. And at the end of the spot, it came up and it said, paid for by the "Don't Let Them Shove Their Religion Down Your Throats Committee." It was actually there on the media spot. And that tells you something about what levers the supporters thought they could pull in the debate that made it seem that any sort of entry into the public realm by religion was somehow inappropriate. So I think that's one way that religion was dismissed in the debate.

The other thing that I think happened is that there were religious voices in Oregon raising the kinds of concerns that I'm raising here about the disadvantaged, about the poor, about the disabled—and they were dismissed, not only because of religion but also for a second reason. Those arguments about the disadvantaged were dismissed because they were interpreted to be mere covers for the real agenda, which was a pro-life agenda.

And I think that's a real mistake, too. I understand why that leap in logic was made, but I think it's important to take these arguments at face value, especially when you think about the fact that in the state of Oregon there's a huge Catholic health care system that offers lots of social services and has their fingers on the pulse on a lot of disadvantaged Oregonians. And to not take seriously those kinds of objections from people who work every day down in the trenches with these problems of poverty and lack of access to health care does the whole debate a real disservice, I think.

Is there any evidence in Oregon that the sorts of problems that you've raised have actually occurred?

On their face, the official reports out of Oregon so far don't seem to indicate that these sorts of problems have occurred. But there are some issues with the reporting that I think are worth mentioning. The law requires doctors to report, and there are penalties in the law for any doctors who don't report. So there are some safeguards there, but it's important to say where they are and where they aren't. For example, all the reports are filled out by physicians—by the attending physicians that are supervising the patient that has requested assisted suicide. So they're not reported by the patient. They're not reported by the families. So the basic demographic information—the objective measures of the patient's age, gender, race, medical diagnosis—I think is probably reliable.

But there are some indications that the more subjective perceptions of physicians—about whether the patient had concerns about finances, pain, depression, being a burden to the family—are less reliable, and these are critical. Of course, these are all problems when you have the physician reporting his or her perception of a patient's condition. In fact, one of the few studies we have to shed some light on this problem shows significant discrepancies between what the family members reported as their perception of the patient's needs in terms of caregiving burdens, pain and financial worries [and what the doctor reported].

Opposition by Disability-Rights Groups

Let's briefly take a look at this from a different angle. Social conservatives often make the argument that physician-assisted suicide devalues life by creating certain classes of people whose lives are possibly no longer worth living. Is there any truth to this argument, and is there any danger that physician-assisted suicide, even if we have universal health care, could ultimately lead to involuntary euthanasia of the severely handicapped or the infirm elderly?

I, like many progressives, am worried about slippery-slope arguments that go too far. At the same time, I don't want to completely dismiss the idea that there can be slippage that happens. Once you take one step, it's easier to take another. I do think that there's something there.

My worry—and I think you'll hear this from a lot of the disability-rights organizations—is that there is the sense that given how hard it is to get health care, given the day-to-day kinds of constraints people with disabilities have to live with, that there is this feeling that society really doesn't value their lives as much as they do able-bodied people. I heard that over and over again from disability-rights activists. And that's a real worry.

Were you surprised by the recent defeat of the physician-assisted suicide bill in California?

I haven't followed that case that closely. But I mentioned the *Los Angeles Times* article that was a sort of post-mortem on the bill there, and one of the things that they said was that one of the pieces that really did get some traction was the argument by disability-rights groups. And what's important about them is that they're not typical, like pro-life groups. They're not a religious group. They don't fall prey to the easy dismissal that sometimes the Oregon Right to Life or the Catholic Church in Oregon fell prey to. And in fact, they're civil liberties defenders, defenders of the Americans with Disabilities Act and other things. And I think for that group to stand up and say, "Hold on a minute, there's something else going on that people aren't seeing"—I think it matters to people.

If you look at the national bodies of the American Medical Association, the American Nurses Association, the American Psychiatric Association, all of them filed amicus briefs in these cases against the legalization of assisted suicide and were worried about its impacts on vulnerable populations. In the American Psychiatric Association's case, undiagnosed depression was a big worry there. So these groups said, look, we think that palliative care really can address most of these issues and some of the reasons why people reach for assisted suicide is to get problems solved that could be reached by better palliative care or better psychiatric care.

Given the different types of opposition against this practice, do you think it is likely that for at least the time being Oregon will remain unique as the only state that allows assisted suicide, or do you think that there's a decent chance that some other state will enact a similar law?

It's hard to prognosticate on these things. New York was one of the earlier states to really think about this pretty seriously, in the mid-1980s. The state even had a task force thinking about it. And in the end, New York ended up saying that regardless of whether we can think about this as a good practice, it's beside the point as long as we have vulnerable patients who might be disproportionately affected. In fact, the way they put it was that the risks of legalizing assisted suicide for vulnerable individuals "in a health care system and society that cannot effectively protect against the impact of inadequate resources and ingrained social disadvantage, are likely to be extraordinary." There's been a concentration of states considering the practice in the upper Northwest, and what those states have in common is that they have ballot initiatives. Where the successes have been, they've sort of bypassed the legislatures and gone through the balloting initiative process where you really can run mass media campaigns. I think if we do see it moving forward, my guess is it's going to be another state with ballot initiatives.

Legalizing Assisted Suicide Would Devalue the Lives of the Disabled and Severely Ill

Teresa Favuzzi

Teresa Favuzzi is executive director of the California Foundation for Independent Living.

For the past few years the *[San Jose] Mercury News* has consistently opined for the legalization of assisted suicide. However, for the third time in as many years, this extreme legislation was rebuked by Democratic and Republican members of the state Legislature. This is not surprising given the vast opposition from over 20 statewide and national disability rights organizations, the California Medical Association, the California Hospice and Palliative Care Association and civil rights organizations like the California League of Latin American Citizens, not to mention groups representing the seniors, the poor and the uninsured.

Even if we look to other states on the issue of assisted suicide, we can track a long string of failures. While it is fairly well-known that Oregon legalized this practice some time ago, 24 other states have rejected it. Each year, the group Compassion & Choices, which descended from the extremist Hemlock Society, attempts legalization, and it continually fails. Its most recent failures to legalize assisted suicide have occurred in Arizona, Hawaii and the very progressive Vermont.

First, opposition to assisted suicide legalization in California remains as strong as ever. A coalition called Californians Against Assisted Suicide was formed in 2005 to oppose this issue, and continues to add new members each year. While the people and organizations in this coalition may not agree on every issue of public policy, we remain strongly united on the opinion that any legalization of assisted suicide is a frightening and potentially disastrous prospect for the people of California. Similar coalitions have been built in the states that have also defeated assisted suicide.

While many legislators, like society in general, may initially view assisted suicide as an acceptable relief to suffering, after learning more about this dangerous proposition . . . they become increasingly opposed to any legalization.

This fact is not lost on those politicians deciding these issues in Sacramento [site of the California legislature]. While many legislators, like society in general, may initially view assisted suicide as an acceptable relief to suffering, after learning more about this dangerous proposition from a diverse array of reputable organizations opposing this practice, they become increasingly opposed to any legalization. Simply put, while people are concerned about caring for those dealing with chronic disease, disability or end-of-life care, they are not willing to permit the prescribing of drugs for the purpose of suicide.

Creating Pressure to Choose Suicide

Further, once we begin prescribing individuals with serious illnesses a lethal dose for a quick out, what message are we sending society about disability, illness, end-of-life issues and the medical profession? The American Medical Association writes in its position regarding assisted suicide, "It is understandable, though tragic, that some patients in extreme duress may come to decide that death is preferable to life. However, allowing physicians to participate in assisted suicide would cause more harm than good. Physician assisted suicide is fundamentally incompatible with the physician's role as healer, would be difficult or impossible to control, and would pose serious societal risks."

Even going beyond the reasons listed above, given California's current health-care crisis and the extreme cost pressures faced by many individuals and families, legalization of assisted suicide would create pressure to opt for assisted suicide. Consider this, especially given the relatively minimal cost of an overdose of pills vs. tens of thousands or hundreds of thousands of dollars for medical care.

Thankfully, voters and legislators have been able to separate the obvious emotional factors surrounding such a heart-wrenching issue and, rather, focus on the significant dangers of legalizing assisted suicide in this society as it operates today. Legislators have also expressed serious concerns over the future of any assisted suicide legalization. Regardless of their personal feelings on this issue, they know nothing can prevent future legislatures from expanding assisted suicide, much as they have in places like the Netherlands where, over 20 years, supposed death with dignity has evolved into full-blown euthanasia.

All of these factors have led to the rejection of assisted suicide legalization. Legislators could continue to push this issue in 2008. However, in my view enough is enough, and the California Legislature should turn its attention fully toward real health-care reform and other serious issues affecting large numbers of Californians. But should bill authors continue to resuscitate this failed issue, I have no doubt that opposition will again be diverse and overwhelming.

Legalizing Assisted Suicide Would Undermine Patients' Trust in Physicians

American Geriatrics Society

The American Geriatrics Society is a nonprofit organization of health professionals devoted to improving the health, independence, and quality of life of all older people.

The American Geriatrics Society [AGS] has previously issued a statement on Physician-Assisted Suicide (PAS) and Voluntary Active Euthanasia (VAE). The public debate on this subject reflects the concerns of many individuals about what will happen in the last phase of their lives. The Society has affirmed that patients have the authority to choose among available plans of care, but their autonomy is limited when there are substantial detrimental effects on the lives of others or their choices conflict with legal or professional standards. Advocates of extending legal and professional standards to include VAE and PAS believe it is the patient's right to choose deliberately to end his or her life, under circumstances of intolerable suffering, when that individual reasonably and voluntarily prefers death to the life that confronts him or her.

Definition of Terms

Physician-assisted suicide: When a physician provides either equipment or medication, or informs the patient of the most efficacious use of already available means, for the purpose of assisting the patient to end his or her own life.

Voluntary active euthanasia: When, at the request of the patient, a physician administers a medication or treatment, the intent of which is to end the patient's life.

Withholding or withdrawing treatment: When a medical intervention is either not given or the ongoing use of the intervention is discontinued, allowing natural progression of the underlying disease state.

Allowing [voluntary euthanasia and physician-assisted suicide] opens the door to abuse of the frail, disabled, and economically disadvantaged of society, by encouraging them to accept death prematurely rather than to burden society and family.

Position

1. For patients whose quality of life and expected lifespan has become so limited as to make earlier death preferable to prolongation of life, the professional standard of care should be that of aggressive palliation [ease] of suffering and enhancement of opportunities for a meaningful life, not that of intentional termination of life. It is morally acceptable for a physician to administer a medication or forgo a treatment calculated to improve the patient's and the family's experience, knowing that this plan of care may have the unintended effect of hastening the patient's death. Good care may include the withholding or withdrawing of any medical intervention as well as the specific palliation of symptoms, even if this shortens a person's life.

2. The patient's request for death should trigger the physician's thorough exploration and understanding of the patient's suffering, the reason the request is being made at that particular time, and a vigorous and sustained effort to relieve the distress.

3. Patients for whom these issues are relevant should be informed of two important facts:

a) profound pain can be relieved with analgesia or sedation, if necessary, and b) patients may choose to forgo any life-prolonging intervention including artificial nutrition and hydration.

Because these issues are often misunderstood, physicians have the responsibility to inform their patients of these alternatives.

4. Laws prohibiting VAE and PAS should not be changed. In giving a patient the means to palliate his or her symptoms, a physician may unavoidably provide the means for suicide (e.g., by prescribing necessary but potentially lethal medications). The law should differentiate between this situation and the intentional participation in the planning and execution of a suicide.

5. If PAS or VAE are legal in any jurisdiction, the AGS contends that the strongest protection for patients to make a choice free of coercion should be in place, and that it should be illegal for professional caregivers to receive financial compensation for assisting in suicide or euthanasia.

Rationale for Continued Prohibition

1. Historically, the fundamental goal of the doctor/patient relationship has been to comfort and to cure. To change the physician's role to one in which comfort includes the intentional termination of life is to alter this alliance and could undermine the trust between physician and patient.

2. Allowing VAE and PAS opens the door to abuse of the frail, disabled, and economically disadvantaged of society, by encouraging them to accept death prematurely rather than to burden society and family.

3. It is the general consensus of the AGS that most individuals who consider PAS or VAE do so out of fear of the dying process. The vast majority of patients can be comfortable (which might require sedation) and poten-

tially could find meaning in the last phase of life and choose to forgo a life-sustaining treatment and accelerate dying. All of these options for care, are already legal. Most would choose to live if they had full confidence that the care system would serve them well. A thorough search for the underlying reason for the request for death may uncover several areas amenable to potential interventions (e.g., undertreated physical symptoms, psychosocial or spiritual crisis, clinical depression, etc.).

4. Legalization of physician-assisted suicide might thwart society's resolve to expand services and resources aimed at caring for the seriously ill, eventually dying patient.

Consequences of Continued Prohibition

1. By prohibiting physicians from participating in VAE or PAS, society is limiting the patient's autonomy to choose his or her mode of death. For a patient who has intractable suffering and a limited life span, who has turned down general sedation, and who wishes to avail him- or herself of the choice to plan or execute his or her own demise, this position statement calls upon physicians to withhold our professional assistance. This seems to be a reasonable balancing of our commitment to securing adequate care for the many patients who would be put at risk of shortened lives if VAE and PAS were made available.

2. A small number of patients will choose this alternative despite our professional non-participation and they may be troubled by losing their doctor's involvement. Nevertheless, to respect the moral commitments of all concerned, physicians must be able to disengage from involvement in this aspect of the patient's plan. The physician should ensure that the patient continues to have access to needed medical care.

Legalized Assisted Suicide Reflects a Biased View of the Disabled

Samuel R. Bagenstos

Samuel R. Bagenstos is a professor of law at Washington University School of Law.

At around the same time that the "Baby Doe" cases [which involved denial of treatment to infants born with serious disabilities] initiated the tactical alliance between disability rights and anti-abortion activists, the two groups began to come together again to oppose physician-assisted suicide and the so-called "right to die." Disability rights activists and right-to-life organizations worked together on a number of prominent cases in the 1980s and 1990s in which people with disabilities sought to exercise the "right" to terminate their own lives. When Dr. Jack Kevorkian began using his "suicide machine" to assist people, many of whom had disabilities, in ending their lives, disability rights activists formed "Not Dead Yet," an organization that opposes assisted suicide and euthanasia from a disability perspective. In most major cases involving "right-to-die" issues—including the [Terri] Schiavo case [concerning a Florida woman on life support whose struggle became a moral and legal battle]—Not Dead Yet has filed briefs arguing that the recognition of such a right threatens the lives and interests of people with disabilities. The views of Not Dead Yet are not representative of those of all disability rights activists, but they nonetheless are an important instance of overlap between disability rights and right-to-life views.

Samuel R. Bagenstos, "Disability, Life, Death and Choice," *Harvard Journal of Law and Gender*, Summer 2006. Copyright © 2006 by the President and Fellows of Harvard College. Reproduced by permission.

Disability Rights Activists' Opposition

As in the "Baby Doe" cases, opponents of abortion object to assisted suicide because it is inconsistent with their understanding of the sanctity of human life. But disability rights activists have again articulated a critique that is distinct from the arguments of the right-to-life movement. In an argument that parallels their position on the "Baby Doe" cases, disability rights activists like those affiliated with Not Dead Yet contend that the practice of assisted suicide reflects a discriminatory belief that life with a disability is not worth living. They further argue that if the law recognizes a "right to die"—no matter how stringently regulated—people with disabilities will be pressured into exercising it.

Disability rights activists argue that if a person without a disability chooses to commit suicide, society treats that choice as the product of an irrational decisionmaking process that should not be given effect. But "when a person 'chooses' death over an 'undignified' life with a disability, the system sympathizes with that individual's plight and supports his right to die, assuming his disability is the root of his supreme despair." That difference, disability rights advocates argue, reflects biases about the "quality of life" experienced by individuals with disabilities. Both medical professionals and nondisabled members of the lay public believe that disability has a more negative effect on life quality than people with disabilities themselves report. People without disabilities thus "readily conclude that the disabled person's wish to die is reasonable because it agrees with their own preconception that the primary problem for such individuals is the unbearable experience of a permanent disability." Their biases can be seen in the "intensely stigmatized language" in which the right-to-die debate proceeds, where "disabled people are defective, damaged, debilitated, deformed, distressed, afflicted, anomalous, helpless and/or infirm," while "nonhandicapped persons are 'normal.'"

Disabled Suffer Social Stigma

In the view of many disability rights advocates, supporters of assisted suicide fail to understand that "the greatest suffering of people with disabilities is the socially stigmatized identity inflicted upon them." Disability rights advocates have long argued that the proper remedy for such stigmatization is not medical treatment to eliminate disabilities—and certainly not medical interventions to eliminate people with disabilities—but is instead guarantees of civil rights to change the hostile and inaccessible aspects of society. "If society alleviated the suffering of facing prejudice," writes Paul Miller, "perhaps life with a disability would be recognized as not only worth living but as valuable as that of anyone else."

Moreover, disability rights advocates who oppose assisted suicide argue that the "choice" by a person with a disability to end her life will rarely be a truly free one. Once recognized, they contend, "the right to die will inevitably become a duty to die. People with major disabilities will be pressured into 'choosing' to end their lives." Free choice in this context may be limited by a physician's advice that is based on inaccurate understandings about the quality of life enjoyed by people with disabilities or erroneous predictions about the future course of an individual's medical condition. It may also be limited by financial pressures, particularly in a world of managed care, and by the related desire not to impose financial or psychological burdens on one's family. And free choice may be limited by the societal stigma attached to disability—stigma that people with disabilities may themselves have internalized:

> [W]hen people with disabilities make a "choice" to seek their right to die, they do so from the position of a society that fears, discriminates against, and stigmatizes disability as undignified. Facing a life of societal exclusion, prejudice, and fear, in conjunction with self-deprecation and devaluation based on those same irrational assumptions, is there really a choice at all?

Importantly, disability rights advocates who have developed the critique of assisted suicide do not believe that there is any regulation that could adequately protect people with disabilities against being coerced into committing suicide. Accordingly, they urge that a flat ban on the practice is necessary. The Supreme Court largely vindicated that position in the [1997] *[Washington v.] Glucksberg* and *Vacco [v. Quill]* cases, which upheld Washington's and New York's absolute bans on assisted suicide.

CHAPTER 2

I Is Assisted Suicide Moral?

Chapter Preface

Whether assisted suicide is moral is a separate issue from that of whether it should be legal. There are some who believe suicide is immoral, yet who also believe that individuals have a right to choose for themselves and should not be prevented from exercising their right by law. There are others who consider it moral in itself but advise against legalizing it because of the possibility that laws permitting assisted suicide would be abused.

Most religions have traditionally held that all human life is sacred and that suicide is therefore immoral. The majority of conservative Christians believe that life is a gift from God so only God should determine when it ends; some of them believe that they would be punished in an afterlife for taking their own lives. However some liberal Christians and some members of other religions consider suicide a moral option for ending suffering, as do many people who have no religious affiliation. In their view, suffering that cannot be relieved is an unqualified evil and therefore, unless a person has a genuine desire to go on living, there is no reason not to seek the same option we provide to sick animals, namely a merciful end to their suffering.

Not everyone who thinks suicide is wrong bases that conviction on religious grounds. Some believe that life, even when it involves suffering, has meaning and that not to wait for life to end naturally would be to deny that any meaning exists. Death, they feel, would be worse than suffering, not only for them personally but because of the impact that making suicide acceptable would have on society.

Assisted-suicide advocates often base their arguments on the moral conviction that each individual has an inherent right to determine his or her own destiny. According to this view, the right to life includes the right to end life, and it is as wrong to deny that right as it is to deprive a person of any other liberty. Suicide is already legal in all states; only assistance in carrying it out is at issue. Opponents point out that the right to take one's own life does not necessarily include a right to receive help from someone else.

Advocates of assisted suicide who support the freedom-of-choice argument qualify it with the statement "as long as it does not harm others." Opponents, however, feel that assisted suicide does harm others and therefore is not moral. In the first place, they claim, it harms the physician and other assistants, who may find preparing for and carrying out the act more troubling than does the patient. In the second place, it affects loved ones, they argue, and in the third place, making it socially acceptable harms ill or disabled people who might not otherwise choose death but who are led to do so because they feel that they are burdens on their families or on society. Supporters of the disabled fear that the right to die might come to be seen as a duty to die.

Yet there are a few bioethicists who think that a duty to die does exist. They argue that it is wrong for terminal patients who need expensive care to drain the resources of their families, and that it may even be wrong for them to draw on health-care funding that could be devoted to others with productive years ahead of them. This is not a common view, but in the future it may gain ground—a possibility that worries those who place a higher value on individual lives than on the collective welfare of society. The authors of the viewpoints in this chapter debate this and other issues surrounding the morality of assisted suicide.

Religious Objections to Assisted Suicide Contradict the Premise of Free Will

Alvaro Vargas Llosa

Alvaro Vargas Llosa is a senior fellow at and director of the Center on Global Prosperity at the Independent Institute and a nationally syndicated columnist for The Washington Post Writers Group.

Apersonal experience recently reaffirmed my conviction that the government, which is sometimes the mechanism by which my next-door neighbor expropriates my free will, should not prolong a person's suffering against his or her own wishes.

A couple of months ago, I underwent surgery. The operation caused traumatic complications that only now, after undergoing surgery for a second time, have started to give way to a process of recovery. For five weeks, I was virtually disabled; I spent my time grappling with excruciating pain and the fear that, if my condition became irreversible, few of my actions in the future would be really free.

A few things kept me going. My wife, who witnessed—but was never paralyzed by—some shocking scenes, was one of them. Also, for reasons that remain mysterious to me, certain literature lifted my spirits when I was able to concentrate. "The Psychiatrist," a short story by Machado de Assis, the 19th-century Brazilian writer, had a therapeutic effect. It is the tale of a physician who locks up an entire town in a mental asylum in the name of science. I also drew inspiration from Albert J. Nock's biography of Thomas Jefferson, which refers to the great American's distrust of the medical profession ("the judicious ... physician should ... (simply assist) the salutary effort which nature makes to re-establish the disordered functions").

But there was one other thing that kept me going: the idea of death as relief. I remember thinking what a powerful psychological effect the legalization of euthanasia would have on suffering patients if they knew that, ultimately, putting a stop to it all with minimal suffering and professional help was an option.

I was not surprised to learn that in Oregon, the only state in the U.S. where assisted suicide has been decriminalized, just 300 patients have taken that route in the last 10 years. In Switzerland, which joins the Netherlands and Belgium as the only countries where assisted suicide is legal, the numbers are proportionately higher—but only because the dignified solution is also open to foreigners.

The religious argument against euthanasia—that it violates the sanctity of life—contradicts the single most powerful premise of the Judeo-Christian tradition: that God gives every person free will.

Other nations—Uruguay, for example, where a judge may pardon a killer if the homicide is "pious" and has been committed with the victim's consent—have allowed sufficient cracks in the legal system to leave the matter open to interpretation. But, for the most part, euthanasia remains a taboo.

Inconsistent Arguments

Two reasons account for this situation. One is a tradition inaugurated by Hippocrates, whose original oath rejected euthanasia. The medical profession continues to swear something similar to that oath today. The second, more important, reason is religious. The Judeo-Christian legacy weighs heavily against euthanasia, although there are proponents of assisted suicide among certain branches of Protestantism, including some Methodists and Episcopalians. Among polytheistic beliefs, Hinduism is also inclined against euthanasia, although in some circumstances a terminally ill person can be assisted because the avatars are thought to be ready to take him.

The religious argument against euthanasia—that it violates the sanctity of life—contradicts the single most powerful premise of the Judeo-Christian tradition: that God gives every person free will. Under a spiritual guise, it amounts to saying that the end—the preservation of a live body that has been rendered useless—justifies the means, prolonging the torment that that body inflicts on the patient's spirit. Finally, it undermines the belief that the spirit outlives the body, conferring sanctity on the useless body rather than on the spirit desperate to liberate itself from the suffering.

Jack Kevorkian, the doctor who assisted with the suicide of terminally ill patients and served eight years in prison for those "crimes," was convicted under a law that never should have been enacted. We would do no good to our civilization if we reacted to Kevorkian's return to society by simply dismissing him as a nutty "has been" or taking refuge in the disgust we may feel at the videotape [of his assisted suicide process] he sent to "60 Minutes" in 1998—the one that triggered his prosecution.

Kevorkian became both a celebrity and a criminal because the law made him one. His reappearance in society reminds us that his uncomfortable cause continues to be just. The quicker the law moves in the direction of justice on this profoundly moral issue, the sooner we will prevent future Kevorkians—both the celebrity types and those who perform clandestine euthanasia in so many countries today.

Religious and Spiritual Principles Lead to Support of Assisted Suicide

Kenneth W. Phifer

Kenneth W. Phifer is minister emeritus of the First Unitarian Universalist Congregation of Ann Arbor, Michigan. He is the author of two books, Hold On: Getting Through Tough Times *and* Becoming at Home in the World.

In the first year of my ministry, an older woman confided in me that she wanted to die. She was weary of pain and helplessness. She felt diminished by being a care-receiver rather than a care-giver. Life had no pleasure or purpose for her other than pain relief. She was without hope. She wanted the release of death and was not even able to help herself accomplish this. It took eight years of misery for her yearning to become reality. My efforts to comfort her were futile, even, as I look back now, cruel.

Some twenty years after that I was involved with a woman in a different congregation I was serving, Merian Frederick, who sought out the services of Dr. Jack Kevorkian. On October 22, 1993, in the presence of her son and daughter-in-law and myself and with the assistance of Dr. Kevorkian, Merian ended her life. Her choice to do so was made after a struggle of several years with ALS ([amyotrophic lateral sclerosis, commonly called] Lou Gehrig's disease) and with the awareness that she would soon lose her only means of communicating with the world, the strength in her fingers to write her thoughts on a yellow pad or tap out a message on her computer.

I had known Merian for twelve years, worked with her in many capacities in the church, and counseled with her and her family on many personal issues. We had often discussed hastened death before she first experienced the symptoms of ALS. Within a few days of her being diagnosed, that conversation became very practical and very personal. As her spiritual counselor, I worked with her to be sure that every possible option was considered and then considered again. Her family was intimately involved in this conversation and in the eventual decision that Merian made.

Had there been a better way for Merian to be relieved of what she viewed as pure hell—a good mind soon to be unable to communicate because of the ruined body in which it was housed—she would have chosen it. Having made her choice she spent the last days of her life more happily and more purposefully than at any time since learning the name and nature of her disease.

To choose death sooner rather than later can be an act of high moral stature. Mere existence is not an absolute value.

Sometimes Life Is Not Worth Living

If I have learned no other lesson from more than thirty years of ministry, I have certainly learned that sometimes life is not worth living.

If we reach that point of suffering and choose to hasten our death, we should have the best available help to make the terminal point of life truly good and gentle for us. This may call for professionals in health care, like doctors or nurses or pharmacists. It is likely to involve family members and/or close friends. Spiritual counseling is also sometimes needed. For some people all of these will be important.

If loved ones and professionals are able and willing to cooperate with us, the moment of our death can truly be full of love.

I support the right of competent individuals to choose a hastened death when the measure of their suffering goes beyond their capacity to endure it. Five religious/spiritual principles inform my support of hastened death.

Mere Existence Is Not an Absolute Value

That which exists changes, grows, deteriorates, becomes something quite different. Value is found more in the process than in the simple existence of any form of life. Conscious and articulate life, human life, sometimes can choose its changes, grounding that choice in values and meanings derived from its own life experiences. Sometimes the change that we choose is death, an end to this existence being preferable to a continuation of it.

Every one of the religions and philosophies that has had a major influence on our society argues this way.

Socrates believed that death was better than violating the law of the city of Athens, to which he had sworn fealty.

Jews perished at Masada rather than be enslaved.

Christians martyred themselves rather than betray their god by bowing to a Roman deity.

There are ideals, values, principles, and persons for which and for whom we would give up our lives if called upon to do so. What parent would not sacrifice his/her own life to save the life of their child? There are people who risk their lives, and sometimes lose them, in rescuing a stranger.

By making such a choice as this, we are at least implicitly saying that our death helps someone who is left behind. In certain circumstances, we may regard that way of helping another as being of higher value than our own existence.

To choose death sooner rather than later can be an act of high moral stature. Mere existence is not an absolute value.

Life Should Be Respected

We should rejoice in life and be glad that we are alive. We should not give up life cheaply or quickly, our own or others.

We should live as fully as we can for as long as we can. But there are different ways of doing this.

My friend Pansy respected life by defying her doctors when they declared that her ninety-six-year-old kidneys had shut down and were not going to function again. Three months after this diagnosis, she went home. She went back to her purposeful work of calling people who were house-bound or in nursing homes and hospitals to cheer them up. She kept this up until her energies gave out a year later and she died.

Those who argue that the deity gives us pain in order to help us grow spiritually or to chastise us for our sinfulness are missing the moral mark.

The Pitney VanDusens also respected life. They loved each other over many years. They made a pact as part of that love that they would die together. When both were of advanced age, and one of them was in very poor health, one day they simply lay down on their marital bed and he took her life and then his own. They made it clear that they did not wish to live under conditions in which they could not give but only take, conditions in which they would only be a burden to others, conditions in which they could only suffer. It was time for them to move on. They respected life by ending it and making room for someone else to enjoy life.

Sometimes choosing to die is as much a sign of respecting life as choosing to live.

No Moral Worth

Those who argue that the deity gives us pain in order to help us grow spiritually or to chastise us for our sinfulness are missing the moral mark. How could anyone have confidence in a deity who would cause the kind of suffering that one can see daily in hospitals, nursing homes, and emergency rooms? Are we to believe that a deity brought to two mothers the anguish of losing their sons to murderers who tortured them, forced them to have sex with each other, and then killed them? Just so the mothers could grow spiritually? What of those young men and the terror and humiliation of their last hours—was that because of their sinfulness? Such views are morally monstrous.

My experience as a chaplain at the Massachusetts Hospital School for Handicapped Children revealed to me the enormous suffering through which some children must go. The various ailments of these youngsters were not the consequence of their moral failings. They were simply damnable bad luck. I could not imagine a divine figure who would bring such anguish to these gutsy boys and girls and their families. That they redeemed their suffering with courage and humor and hard work did not make me or them grateful for their pain and disability. It only made me and others more appreciative of their endurance and their achievements.

Suffering that we have not chosen does not in and of itself have any moral value. Disease, accident, decline, great age do not themselves have moral worth. How we face them does. One ethical way of doing that is by choosing not to let that suffering continue when it is of such magnitude that nothing else in life matters and there is no hope of relief save in death.

Suffering is not itself moral. Only our response to it can be moral.

Autonomy is necessary if we are to have meaning as moral creatures.

Respecting Individuals' Autonomy

Within the constraints of time and place and ability, each of us can choose how to live and each of us should be allowed to choose how we die. It is not so much that we have a right to die, as it is that, if death does not surprise us, we have a right to choose the moment of our letting go.

Autonomy is essential in moral action. Autonomy means that we are informed about the conditions in which we find ourselves and that we have legitimate options among which to choose. Autonomy does not mean that we are coerced subtly or overtly into one decision or another. It means that we freely make the choice we deem best.

There is no principle in modern medical practice more important than this one. The idea of informed consent—required for treatment and for research involving human beings—is grounded in the notion of autonomy. The individual whose life or health is at stake should decide what should and should not be done to her, not the doctor or the nurse or the family. Their role is to inform and support the individual in his or her free choice. From the Nuremberg Code onward, this value of respecting the autonomy of each person by obtaining informed consent before initiating a medical or experimental procedure has been recognized as a fundamental value.

No less should this be true in making decisions that will hasten death: not starting treatment, stopping treatment, treating pain even if the consequence is a more rapid death, actively helping to bring about death.

Autonomy is necessary if we are to have meaning as moral creatures. It must be as applicable in our waning days and hours as it is when we are in full strength.

Individuals Are Embedded in Community

It is in the connections that we make to others that the deepest layers of meaning in our lives are revealed. We make these connections with families, friends, colleagues, neighbors, people who share our religious or political outlook or who enjoy the same sport or hobby. We also make connections with people who are different from us and who in their difference call upon us to enlarge our vision of the human collective.

In all the major decisions of our living, thinking about and sharing with a wider network of associations is important for understanding the larger meaning of what we are choosing to do.

This is especially true when it comes to a decision about ending our lives. It is of great importance that we begin now to talk with those we care about regarding our feelings about death and dying. How long do we wish to live when our condition is terminal and our suffering great? Such talk helps us to know the impact of our decisions about how we want to die on those who survive us. In loving relationships, this knowledge may sometimes, and rightly, influence the choices we make.

Preparing an Advance Medical Directive and a Medical Durable Power of Attorney helps to clarify our views at this moment. Such documents announce to loved ones and strangers how we wish to confront our ending. Together with conversation, these papers help others to understand, even if they do not agree with us, why we have made the decision we have made.

What right has any one of us, much less society at large, to force people to endure grievous pain that cannot be relieved short of total unconsciousness?

Death and dying are in one sense the most individual and isolating events of our lives. But in another sense these moments are communal. The dying and death of any person we love touches us, changes us, alters the way life is for us. The presence at memorial services of physicians, nurses, and other health care workers and care-givers testifies to the fact that those who are with us professionally in our last days are also part of our community.

No one is an island. The death of any of us affects all who know that person. How that death occurs is often as significant as the fact of death.

We live and die in community. . . .

Doctors Cannot Always Be Healers

Hastened death has always been a part of human societies. It is a more urgent issue today because of medical knowledge and technology. Where pain can be relieved, it should be. Where healing can occur, we can all be glad.

But the truth is that not all pain can be managed. What right has any one of us, much less society at large, to force people to endure grievous pain that cannot be relieved short of total unconsciousness with no hope that this can be changed? If a person in such a condition pleads for death, as some of us might do, by what moral standard do we continue to refuse to give them the help they are begging for?

A kind system of health care would recognize that different people will make different choices in these agonizing circumstances. A kind system of health care would make provision for all possible choices: risky experimental procedures, hospice care, adequate pain management, and aid in dying for those who choose it.

Furthermore, doctors cannot always be healers. Each of us will come to a point in life when no medical treatment will help us, save perhaps to relieve our pain. At that point, when our condition is terminal, what we need more than anything else is intelligent compassion. We need people who understand the pain in our bodies and the suffering in our souls. Compassion may well be to give us drugs and apply therapies to make our bodies feel better. But for some of us, compassion may well be to help ease us into death.

Doctors already do this, and do it legally and with the support of most religious communities. What they do is act under the principle of the double effect. The double effect is the principle by which doctors prescribe for pain even though they know that the level of medication prescribed will kill the patient. No less an opponent of active hastened death than Pope John Paul II has put his seal of moral approval on the double effect. "It is licit," he writes in The Gospel of Life. ". . . to relieve pain by narcotics, even when the result is decreased consciousness and a shortening of life."

This is a kindness for those whose bodies are racked with pain, whose spirits are sore with despair, who have no realistic hope this side of the grave, and who want relief from their suffering. They want out of life. It is a kindness for the families who suffer watching helplessly as their loved ones writhe in agony.

Ultimately the question of how we die is a spiritual issue, not a medical or legal one. Religious leaders and other counselors can help people to think clearly about the options available. We can give full emotional, moral, and spiritual support to whatever decision the person before us makes. Our responsibility is to be with people, not tell them what they must do or judge them because their decisions do not agree with ours.

The ultimate goal is to enable every person not carried away by sudden death to make informed choices about what happens to them in the last stages of life. We will not all choose the same way. There must be room for those who choose to live even in the face of frightful pain and suffering and for those who choose a hastened death. In this way it becomes possible for each of us to find that even death can be meaningful.

A Just Reorganization of World Health-Care Resources Could Lead to a Duty to Die

Margaret Pabst Battin

Margaret Pabst Battin is a professor of philosophy and medical ethics at the University of Utah and the author of many books. She is a noted proponent of assisted suicide.

I s there a duty to die? This inflammatory question, often originally attributed to then-Governor of Colorado Richard Lamm, was being explored some years ago within the context of American health care, but lately has dropped out of sight—whether because it seemed to have no purchase in the light of new, globalized issues about justice in health care, or because the conclusion was so unpalatable it is hard to [say]. In either case, I want to revive it. Why? Simple. If the strongest argument for the existence of a duty to die, rooted in [medical ethicist] Norman Daniels' early Rawlsian [based on the justice as fairness ideas of philosopher John Rawls] reconstruction, is supplemented by [philosopher] Allen Buchanan's distinctive approach to issues of international justice, it is possible that a new, stronger duty to die might emerge from his conjunction. If so, we ought to recognize it, however difficult that might be; and if not, we still ought to recognize what might lead to its coming to be the case. This "duty to die" is, I predict, sneaking up on us as we explore multilateralist, cosmopolitan accounts of global relations.

In some familiar senses, we already recognize a variety of "duties to die"—including obligations to allow oneself to die, to risk dying, to let oneself be killed, or kill oneself—in a wide range of traditional circumstances. Some of these are role-dependent—for example in military and police services, medical services that may involve exposure to deadly communicable diseases during times of plague or contemporary viruses, or the spy with secret information. Some are less so: rescue missions and capital punishment, for example. Duties to die or to allow oneself to die are sometimes put forward as obligations in religious traditions, for example in Buddhist obligations of self-sacrifice or in the Catholic "higher way" of allowing oneself to die or be killed rather than have an abortion or kill another human being even in self-defense. But the particular duty to die at issue here is one based in distributive issues, where it is considerations of justice and equality that motivate the claim that one better-off party may have a duty to die to enhance the prospects of a worse-off one.

People in rich countries live far longer, far healthier lives, and die much, much later than people in poor parts of the globe.

The issue of whether there is a distributively based duty to die has been argued both as a personal issue and as a societal one. Dan Callahan, who in *Setting Limits* and his later books set the stage for the discussion by calling for restraint on the part of the elderly in the use of life-prolonging medicine, developed a view that would appear to underwrite a passive, though not active, duty to die. Some years later, drawing in part on work by Norman Daniels, I posed the question of the duty to die in an impersonal, social context about the choices one might rationally make under conditions of moderate scarcity in access to health care. More recently, John Hardwig has posed the same question again in the highly personal context of a troubling rumination about duties to his own family— duties he says he willingly accepts not to burden them with obligations of excessive expense or care as he succumbs to extreme old age or terminal illness. It is Hardwig who has made the argument most vivid. But neither Callahan nor Daniels nor Hardwig nor I have explored the question in a still larger context, that context in which it may seem to be both least persuasive to some but most troubling to others. This is the context of global justice.

Global Differences in Life Expectancy

Is there a duty to die? Consider the stark differences in life expectancy around the world. In the rich, industrially developed nations, where human development indices are high, average life expectancy at birth ranges roughly between 72–80 for both sexes, with Japan, Canada, Iceland, Australia, and the Netherlands at the top end of the range. In the poorest, not-yet-developed agrarian nations of the so-called third world, where human development indices are low, life expectancy ranges downward from 60 to 40, and in some countries, like Malawi, Zambia, Mozambique, Zimbabwe, and Sierra Leone, at 40 or below. A child born in Sierra Leona today has a life expectancy of just 34.5 years. Although life expectancy has been increasing in most nations, in some, like Russia in the post-Soviet years, it has been plummeting, down from 69.2 in the five-year period 1985–90 to an estimated 64.4 for 1995–2000, with men dropping to 58.0.

There are also stark global differences in access to health care. The high-income countries (those with per capita annual incomes above $8,500) get almost all the health care made available in the world. In 1994, for example, the rich countries accounted for 89% of global health expenditures, even though they comprise only 16% of the global population. The United States has 5% of the global population, but accounts for 50% of health spending. Furthermore, of the estimated 1.4 trillion disability-adjusted years of life that were lost to disease in that year, the inhabitants of the rich nations suffered just 7% of them. People in rich countries live far longer, far healthier lives, and die much, much later than people in poor parts of the globe.

Can these differences serve to raise a question about a duty to *die*? Perhaps, like most other readers of these remarks, you will reject the question out of hand, even if moved by the plight of distant peoples around the globe. A *duty* to die? While life expectancies may be unequal, you will no doubt say, this hardly establishes that they are inequitable, or that those with longer lifespan expectancies have any duty to those with short life expectancies to even things out. . . . No doubt you will agree that it is unfortunate that inhabitants of the poor countries receive less health care, experience much worse health, and lose far more years of life; but even if you grant that it is unfortunate, you will be less likely to see it as unfair, and in any case you almost certainly do not think that global differences in patterns of life expectancy can impose a duty to *die* on the residents of more fortunate nations.

However, if we look at the various arguments that Callahan, Daniels, Hardwig and I have made directly or indirectly about whether there might be a duty to die in what we all assumed was a Western, first-world, American context, we may see that when supplemented by a plausible additional premise, these arguments have implications reaching far beyond our borders—implications yielding troubling results in a global context—and perhaps bad news for you and me. . . .

Hardwig's Argument

Hardwig argues that an individual who is terminally ill or in need of extensive care may have a duty not only to decline this care, but to die, in order to avoid imposing overly heavy burdens of care and support on family members or loved ones—even if they would willingly bear these burdens. This duty Hardwig sees as stronger for people who are older and who have already lived full lives, especially if they are facing dementing disease like Alzheimer's or Huntington's, whose loved ones have had difficult lives or have already made sacrifices for them; in such conditions, they can no longer hope to make significant contributions to the lives of their loved ones. An individual in this situation—and Hardwig clearly accepts the prospect that he may someday find himself in this position—ought to be willing to die in order to avoid "stealing the futures" of his loved ones, who would otherwise shoulder duties of care to him, rather than buying a little more time for himself.

It is not clear how voluntary choices of an earlier death ... would have real impact on global differences in life expectancy.

This is a complex argument, one that has generated vigorous controversy. But given that it addresses obligations only to immediate family members and loved ones who are directly and severely affected by one's remaining alive, Hardwig's argument would seem to have no implications concerning distant peoples, remote residents of the world whom one does not know, with whom one does not interact, and who inhabit utterly different cultural, social, and religious spheres from one's immediate family. ... While we think it might be a good thing, a decent thing to contribute some of one's assets to help these unfortunate people, there is certainly no duty to sacrifice one's life.

Battin's Argument, Drawing on Daniels

My own argument about the duty to die has not been driven by sentiments of affection or concern for family members, nor is it confined to the orbit of the intimate family situation. Rather, one might say, this argument has been driven by cold self-interest, at least of a theoretical sort. I had claimed that rational self-interest maximizers ... choosing principles that would govern a society characterized by moderate scarcity of health-care resources, would (as Norman Daniels had argued, recognize that health-care resources spent earlier in life—that is, on people in younger age groups—would both be more efficient and would raise the chances of survival in early life (a precondition for later life), thus (except in the first generation of such a policy) enhancing one's chances of longer, better survival at a later stage of life. . . . At a minimum, this would mean—as Callahan and Hardwig both see—refraining from demanding or accepting expensive, high-tech health care—not only respirators, tubes, and machines, but elaborate diagnostic procedures, prolonged hospitalization, and so on—in a last-ditch effort to prolong their lives. But if there were a duty to refrain from using resources in terminal illness or extreme old age that might be more justly allocated to the care of younger people, I then argued, given the potentially cruel consequences of living without adequate care, many rational self-interest maximizers . . . would welcome social policies recognizing elective assisted suicide or active voluntary euthanasia—not obligatory or forced, not age-tagged, and certainly not secret, but available for those who might choose them. Thus there would not be a duty to cause oneself to die, but if there were an obligation to refrain from receiving care, causing oneself to die rather than merely being disenfranchised from care might seem the preferable choice. . . .

This argument too may seem to have little or no relevance to the global context. After all, it is not clear how voluntary choices of an earlier death, including those involving physician-assisted suicide or physician-performed euthanasia, even if supported by social practices and expectations, would have real impact on global differences in life expectancy. Drawing on data from the Netherlands, we can expect that such choices, at least as made in a current world in which they are legally tolerated and fairly widely socially accepted, would mean forgoing only the last few weeks of life, that only comparatively few people would make them, and that the savings in health-care costs would be modest. . . . Savings would have comparatively little impact on overall health-care costs even in a developed nation that permitted assisted dying, and virtually no discernible impact on global differences in life expectancy of people in poor countries.

Callahan's Argument

Dan Callahan also employs arguments that, in their origins, are sympathetic to Daniels' view of age-rationing. Callahan's initial view was that the elderly should rethink the meaning of old age and refrain from claiming expensive health-care resources in an attempt to prolong life indefinitely; he has expanded this view to insist that all of us reinspect our assumptions about health, disease, aging, and death, and abandon our relentless pursuit of medical "progress" in general, not only in old age. We must stop assuming that we can conquer all disease, or indefinitely prolong life, and turn things over to the generation after us.

Nothing . . . [we] might do in shortening our lives or letting them be shorter would seem to affect the welfare of people in distant countries.

Does Callahan think there is a duty to die? He is staunchly opposed to any direct ending of life, and would certainly deny that there is any "duty to die" in the sense accepted straightforwardly by Hardwig or partially and obliquely by myself. However, he recognizes that the rethinking of cultural assumptions about medical progress and the meaning of life will often mean that death arrives earlier, and he clearly recognizes obligations in connection with the approach of death: this is a "passive" duty, the duty of restraint, an obligation to refrain from claiming expensive health-care resources that might postpone death and prolong one's life—but a duty nevertheless.

Of these three discussions of duties at the end of life, Callahan's alone is sensitive to global issues in health. He holds that greater equality in health circumstances ought to be brought about around the world. But he sees this simply as a matter of holding back in the first world from our unthinking dedication to so-called medical progress, holding back in a way that will allow us to achieve a "steady state" medicine, allowing the developing world to gradually catch up with the developed world so that global health-care equality will be more nearly achieved. But, like Hardwig, Daniels, and Battin, Callahan does not explore the more direct obligations that his view might seem to support. . . .

Nothing Hardwig or Callahan or I or Daniels, for that matter, might do in shortening our lives or letting them be shorter would seem to affect the welfare of people in distant countries, or in any way serve to decrease the disparity between their life spans and ours. Arguing that John or Dan or Norm or I or, for that matter, you, the reader of this paper, ought to die a little earlier to extend the lifespans of people in the poorer nations of Africa or Asia or Latin America may seem just as futile as insisting that we eat all the food on our plates to keep people from starving in Somalia or Sudan or whatever is our current Armenia. . . .

Is there a "global" duty to die, a distributively based duty to end one's life or let it end for reasons of global health equity? It seems that the answer is *no*.

But I think this answer lets us off the hook a bit too quickly. Neither Hardwig's vivid and disturbing reflections nor Battin's Daniels-flavored argument nor Callahan's thoughtful perceptions about the state of American health care appear to found a satisfactory argument about a duty to die, whether positive or negative, direct or indirect, that has any purchase in a global context. Just the same, exposing assumptions central to these arguments and then exposing these assumptions to globalist critique may suggest that they could, on the contrary, be stretched to global scope. . . .

The Missing Link

If global health care were indeed an interactive, interrelated global system, whether based in nation-states or other administrative bodies, and if the appropriate redistributive structures were in place, . . . tiny savings from first-world choices of earlier death would prove far more efficient in protecting and extending life in the third world: the costs of one expensive and not very effective unit of life-prolonging care in the first world, say a week in intensive care on life support, buys many, many units of inexpensive and highly effective care in the second and especially third: oral rehydration, vaccination, basic reproductive health care. This is just the point about savings and efficiency that is so central to the redistributive claims here. Health-care-relevant institutions of this sort would enable savings in health-care costs in one generation and in one area of the globe to enhance life expectancy in younger generations in areas where it is now shorter—future Ugandans, for example—an effort that would (except in the first generation of such a policy) serve the interests of all. . . .

Thus this argument depends on the existence of redistributive structures that function on a global scale, making it possible for savings in the first world to serve as resources in the third. We do not have these structures yet—at least, not in full. . . .

With this "missing link" in place—a set of global, health-related, redistributive structures against a background of interrelated obligations of mutual health-related support in a cooperative scheme involving some form or other of a closed system—. . . the conditions would be satisfied within which a "duty to die" would become a reality. This duty would be the duty to conserve health-care resources by foregoing treatment or directly ending one's life in the interests of justice in health care, and it would be reflected in more nearly equal health prospects and life expectancies around the globe. . . . Perhaps it might even amount to something stronger than merely a duty to cease consuming medical resources; a positive duty to die, at least if the development of a global system of health care, responsive to a wide range of cultural values, involved radical changes in attitudes toward life prolongation and the meaning of extended illness or old age. This is what I was concerned with at the outset—whether even as the issue of the "duty to die" seemed to have dropped out of sight as issues about justice in global health have come to the fore, that a new, stronger duty to die might emerge. I think it could. Those who argue in their various ways as Hardwig, Battin in drawing on Daniels, and Callahan do may well be committed to the conclusion that having one's death occur earlier, whether directly caused or as the result of refraining from claiming expensive life-prolonging care, would even in a global world be the morally right thing—indeed, the globally just thing to do.

The good news is that as global inequalities in life expectancy are reduced, the obligation envisioned here becomes less and less burdensome.

However, . . . this is true at the moment only in theory. It is *not* possible as a matter of actual practice under current global conditions. How could "we," the global rich, translate savings from our own earlier demises into health gains for "them," the global poor? Charity, yes, but genuine reallocation, no. And how could "their" restraint in traditional health-affecting practices be organized so that it improved "our" health without making "them" still worse off? Thus while we in the first world cannot now have a global duty to die—

whether by declining life-prolonging care or ending life in more direct ways—in order to promote lifespan equity among the inhabitants of the world, we certainly do . . . have an obligation to promote international structures of transfer and redistribution of health-care savings, against a background of mutual health-related obligations, which would mean that choices concerning dying in the first world would directly affect life-prospects in the second and third. Similarly, while they—the inhabitants of the poor nations of the globe—cannot now have a duty to us, the rich, to refrain from health-affecting practices that compromise first-world health, like forest-cutting and field-burning and bush-meat-eating, they too could come to do so in the future.

Here, then, is the message for the future: First and foremost, though I have not argued for it here: the overall disparity between global rich and global poor must be reduced dramatically. But failing this, what needs to be built are the structures for a world in which my health prospects affect yours and yours affect mine, so that we all come to have a mutual interest in making both of our prospects better. . . . Thus this argument is not so much about the duty to die in itself, but about noticing what hugely important social institutions just aren't there, and recognizing our obligation to create them. The emergence of the duty to die would be a kind of epiphenomenon, so to speak, a symptom that we're getting these institutions in place.

Is this overall argument a *reductio ad absurdum* of the Hardwig, Daniels, Battin, and Callahan views, or a genuine conclusion, albeit, . . . an extremely demanding one? I'd like to predict that with time, and with growing recognition of the interconnectedness of the interests of the various peoples of the globe (including not only our obligations to other peoples but their obligations to us), we will come to see it not as a silly thought experiment, but as a real challenge to our moral selves to work to develop global health-related structures that form an effective, efficient closed system. It might seem to be bad news for those of us in the fortunate situations of the developed world now enjoying long lifespans, especially since the gains from such savings cannot be realized in the first generation, but, ... it would promote the good of us all by producing a far more just health-related world in the long run. In the bargain we would see extended life expectancies in future generations for all. The good news is that as global inequalities in life expectancy are reduced, the obligation envisioned here becomes less and less burdensome, and may even seem to disappear as appropriate health-care structures are in place and life expectancies even out.

Assisted Suicide Violates Christian Beliefs About Human Life

Albert Mohler

Albert Mohler is the president of the Southern Baptist Theological Seminary. He is also a commentator and host of a daily live nationwide radio program and writes a popular blog.

Anne Lamott is a writer of incredible honesty and uncommon candor. Beyond this, she is a highly gifted artist, writing with a fluid and passionate style that attracts readers who quickly feel drawn into Lamott's life and experiences.

Additionally, Anne Lamott is a zealous proponent of her own personal causes. Passionately liberal, she is known for her fervent support of abortion on demand (she recently wrote of women whose lives were "righted and redeemed" by *Roe v. Wade*) [the 1973 Supreme Court decision legalizing abortion]. Yet, at the same time, she has managed to identify herself in some sense as a Christian writer, and she describes her own mode of Christian discipleship in terms of being "Jesusy." She has become something of a literary icon among mainline Protestants and leftward evangelicals. Now, however, she appears to be launching out into previously uncharted territory.

Writing in the June 25, 2006 edition of *The Los Angeles Times*, Lamott begins with these words: "The man I killed did not want to die, but he no longer felt he had much of a choice." The language is truly shocking, and Lamott obviously intends to catch the attention of readers when she speaks of "the man I killed." If it is attention she wants, she is almost sure to get more than she intended.

An Assisted Suicide

In her essay, "At Death's Window," Lamott traces her involvement in the assisted suicide of a close friend. She introduces him as having "gone from being tall and strapping, full of appetites and a brilliant manner of speech, to a skeleton, weak and full of messy needs." Lamott's poetic description of her friend's plight underlines the tragedy of his illness.

As Lamott traces his decline, the man who "had always been passionately literary" was losing his ability to read or write. No longer able to travel, hike, or share cherished experiences with his wife, he was only sixty when he was diagnosed with cancer.

The man Lamott helped to die is not identified with his real name. Instead, Lamott refers to the man and his wife as "Mel" and "Joanne." Refusing aggressive chemotherapy treatment, Mel "wanted to feel as well as he could for as long as he could," Lamott recounts, in order to "savor his family and friends and the beauty of life, on his own terms, in the strange basket of sickness."

As is so often the case, the specter of precipitous physical decline accompanied by pain was a real concern. As the prescribed opiates no longer seemed to cover his pain, Lamott told Mel over lunch one day that "if he ever experienced too much pain or diminishment, I would try to help him die on his own terms, if he wanted." ...

The Christian understanding of humanity insists that we are not autonomous creatures that have the right to determine when we shall live and when we shall die.

Clearly, Anne Lamott is enthusiastic about the process. As she recalls her lunchtime conversation with Mel, Lamott recalled that she had not premeditated making her offer. She also recounted the experience she shared with her brothers when they contemplated assisting their own father to die, even as he was slipping away from them due to the ravages of brain cancer. "Two months before he died, when he lay in a hospital bed in our one-room cabin in what amounted to a coma," Lamott recalls, "my younger brother and I crushed up some barbiturates that his doctor had given him to help him sleep, but we couldn't do it. We were too young." Now older, Lamott was apparently ready to act when it came to her friend Mel. When Mel asked Lamott about her understanding of death, she spoke of having heard an Eastern mystic "say that it was like slipping out of a pair of shoes that had never fit very well."

Christians Disagree Among Themselves

The most revealing section of Lamott's essay is this: "Mel was sort of surprised that as a Christian I so staunchly agreed with him about assisted suicide. I believed that life was a kind of Earth school, so even though assisted suicide meant you were getting out early, before the term ended, you were going to be leaving anyway, so who said it wasn't OK to take an incomplete in the course?"

In the economy of just a few words, Lamott effectively turns the Christian understanding of life and death on its head.

No wonder Mel was "sort of surprised" that Lamott, identifying herself as a Christian, would agree to participate in an assisted suicide with such enthusiasm. Christianity teaches a distinctive understanding of human life. At the onset, the Bible reveals that we are not the lords of our own lives in the first place. Life is a gift, and human life is a special gift given to the only creatures who are made in God's own image. We are, in effect, the only sentient beings able to ponder the meaning of our own lives and the reality of our own death. The Christian understanding of humanity insists that we are not autonomous creatures that have the right to determine when we shall live and when we shall die. To the contrary, our lives are in the disposition of the Creator, and human life is understood to possess inherent dignity from its natural beginning until its natural end. Any affirmation of assisted suicide or any form of euthanasia as a way of "releasing" persons by voluntary or involuntary intervention is a rejection of God's sovereign prerogative and a denial of His providence as gracious, merciful, and righteous.

Furthermore, Christianity does not teach that life is just "a kind of Earth school." To the contrary, Christianity affirms the inherent dignity and meaning of our earthly lives. Life is not a course we are taking, so much as it is a stewardship of a priceless gift. It is profoundly true that Christianity points to eternal life beyond this earthly life as the realm of our ultimate existence as believers, but we are not invited to "take an incomplete" in the course of life as we may choose.

As Anne Lamott continues her story, she tells of Mel reminding her of her offer. "I won't be me for much longer," he said. Having communicated with the Hemlock Society (a group that ardently supports euthanasia and offers advice to those wishing to die or to assist someone to die), Lamott "knew exactly how many Seconal pills it took to kill a big person." As she recalls, she knew how to crush the pills and add them to applesauce, and then feed them to the sick person, along with toast and tea so that the pills would not be rejected.

Shortly thereafter, Lamott used what she describes as "wily and underground ways" to amass a sufficient number of Seconal pills to constitute a lethal dose. "That night, Mel and I had a cryptic phone conversation. 'I got it,' I said, like a spy, or a drug dealer."

Disregard of Christian Moral Tradition

A month later, Lamott shared dinner with Joanne and Mel and, along with another friend, listened to his favorite music and told favorite stories. "He was absolutely clear as a bell, brilliant as ever," she remembers. Using the full power of her descriptive ability, she wrote of the air smelling "faintly of honey and laundry, and illness."

Lamott effectively jettisons Christian concern for the preservation of life and dismisses centuries of Christian conviction on the questions of life and death.

After dinner, Mel changed into comfortable pajamas and got into his bed, "wasted, sad, sweet and comfortable." Lamott then went to the kitchen to get the pills, and then made the deadly applesauce "in a tiny Asian bowl."

After eating the applesauce, Mel thanked his friends and wife, and "told us how much he loved his life, and how he wished he could live with us forever." Finally: "After a while, Mel looked around, half smiled and fell asleep. People got up to stretch, for wine or water, or to change albums. He breathed so quietly, for so long, that when he finally stopped, we all strained to hear the sound."

Those words end Lamott's essay. There is no extended moral argument for her action in assisting the suicide of her friend. There is no engagement with the Christian moral tradition, and there is no real sense of moral reflection at all. As with the issue of abortion, Anne Lamott is simply guided by her own sense of what is right and wrong.

With the ease of an author beginning to write on a clean sheet of paper, Lamott effectively jettisons Christian concern for the preservation of life and dismisses centuries of Christian conviction on the questions of life and death. She describes herself as a Christian, but there is nothing even remotely Christian, in any distinctive sense, to be found in her essay on a matter as serious as ending a man's life.

When Anne Lamott writes of "the man I killed" like this, she willingly enters uncharted terrain and forges a brave new morality, embracing assisted suicide as a moral good.

Mel was rightly shocked that a Christian would be such a staunch supporter of assisted suicide. Will Lamott's Christian readers be equally shocked to read of her views now? Those views led directly to Mel's poisoned applesauce.

The Wish to Die Is Based on Social as Well as Medical Issues

Adrienne Asch

Adrienne Asch is a noted bioethicist and authority on the rights of the disabled. She is a professor at the Wurzweiler School of Social Work in New York.

Thanks to the sustained efforts of scholars, clinicians, and grassroots citizen groups like Compassion in Dying, both clinical practice and case law recognize that ill or dying patients and their intimates often are concerned about their experiences and relationships during whatever time they have left to live, not merely with how long they might be maintained by medications, feeding tubes, and breathing machines. Disability activists and lobbying groups such as Not Dead Yet or Americans Disabled for Attendant Programs Today (ADAPT) also espouse the goals of creating and maintaining opportunities for ill, disabled, or dying people to enjoy fulfilling, meaningful relationships, activities, and experiences for however much time they will live. Compassion in Dying and Not Dead Yet differ in their policy and practice goals for two reasons: they focus on different kinds of paradigm cases, and they have profoundly different understandings of how illness and disability affect life's meaning and rewards. The typical case for the misnamed "right to die" movement is an elderly man or woman in the final stages of an inevitably terminal illness, who will soon die regardless of how much medical treatment is invested in his or her last days or weeks. The case that fuels the disability rights movement is that of a relatively young person with a disability, who could live for several years with the condition, but who instead asks to die—as in [the movie] *Million Dollar Baby*, and as in many real-life cases.

Disability Does Not Mean Low Quality of Life

Although mainstream reformers have criticized the way professionals often dealt with patients and their families, the mainstream has too often accepted medicine's view that illness and disability inevitably diminish life's quality. In contrast, disability theorists and activists point to research demonstrating that people with physical, sensory, and cognitive impairments can and do obtain many satisfactions and rewards in their lives. When people with illness and disability report dissatisfaction and unhappiness, they link their distress not to physical pain or to reliance on medications, dialysis, or ventilators, but to those factors that also trouble nondisabled people—problematic relationships, fears about financial security, or difficulties in playing a valued work or other social role.

Disability theorists and activists endorse the growth of hospice, palliative care, pain relief, and greater attention to the psychological and social needs of patients and their loved ones; however, they argue that endorsing treatment withdrawal from people simply because their health or their capacities are impaired undermines the goals of human dignity, patient self-respect, and quality of life. Such goals are best achieved by helping people discover that changed health status and even impaired cognition need not rob life of its value. Respect for self-determination and human dignity entails a commitment to fostering the activities, experiences, and relationships that enrich an individual's life by finding techniques and resources to use those capacities that remain. In the case of Elizabeth Bouvia, a woman disabled by cerebral palsy and painful arthritis who sought aid in dying, the California Court of Appeals supported her request to end her life by focusing on her limitations, pointing to her physical immobility and her need for assistance with tasks like eating and toileting. Although the court described her as "alert" and "feisty," it also characterized her as "subject to the ignominy, embarrassment, humiliation and dehumanizing aspects created by her helplessness." The 1996 court decision that supported physician-assisted suicide in *Washington v. Glucksberg* was filled with similar portrayals of life with impairment: it referred to people who are in a "childlike state" of helplessness, as exemplified by physical immobility or by their use of diapers to deal with incontinence.

Societal tolerance of death for people who could live for months or years with disabilities stems from misunderstanding, fear, and prejudice.

The disability critics of the California court decision revealed an entirely different side to the Elizabeth Bouvia story. They focused on her remaining capacities and on the social and economic problems that contributed to her isolation and depression. . . .

Tolerance of Death for Disabled

Fortunately, some respected mainstream scholars have acknowledged that societal tolerance of death for people who could live for months or years with disabilities stems from misunderstanding, fear, and prejudice. Excerpts from one clinician-philosopher's recent reflections demonstrate a new receptivity to the disability critique of typical end of life practice and policy. . . .

In his 1979 book *Taking Care of Strangers*, Robert Burt exposed the common discomfort of health care professionals in the presence of patients with very significant impairments: "Rules governing doctor-patient relations must rest on the premise that anyone's wish to help a desperately pained, apparently helpless person is intertwined with a wish to hurt that person, to obliterate him from sight." Speaking of a burned and very disfigured patient, Burt contended: "He is a painful, insistent reminder to others of their frailty, an acknowledgement that, in the routine of everyday life, is ordinarily suppressed. Others cannot avoid wishing that he, and his unwanted lesson, would go away. He cannot avoid knowing this of others and wishing it for himself."

These insights should prompt clinicians and policymakers to question how truly autonomous is anyone's wish to die when living with changed, feared, and uncertain physical impairments that lead to anguish and to interpersonal struggles with the very professionals, family members, and friends who are assumed to be supports in a time of trouble. The spirit of such observations illustrates the danger of relying on a simple notion of patient autonomy when deciding to withdraw life-sustaining treatment.

Consider this case from the end of life literature, reported by M. Edwards and Susan Tolle: Their patient—conscious, alert, with mobility impairments that had lasted for forty years—had recently developed breathing problems that necessitated use of a ventilator, which rendered him unable to speak. Finding this increased disability intolerable, he sought death, and family, professionals, and the hospital ethics committee concurred with his autonomous wish. Edwards and Tolle proposed a seven-step procedure to assure themselves that such an aided death is acceptable. Absent from their analysis is any exposure to or contact with people who have more than two weeks of experience living as ventilator users. The case description provides no information on how effectively this patient was communicating (whether by writing, pointing to letters and words, or using a communication technology). It contains no information about whether this man's decision was affected by concerns over how his relationships with family and friends might be changed by his different means of communication. Presumably these clinicians knew that nonvocal but conscious and responsive individuals have been able to interact in family and work settings. One wonders why these clinicians did not urge such means upon this patient before acceding to his pleas for death rather than life without speech. He may have been psychologically abandoned by his family and clinicians when he most needed their energy, resourcefulness, and imagination to help him devise a new way to express himself.

> *What needs to change is not the patient's physical or cognitive situation, but the emotional and interpersonal environment.*

Oregon Suicides Illustrate Social Issues

The most recent report on the workings of Oregon's law on physician-assisted suicide offers yet another illustration of social rather than medical issues at work in requests for assisted dying. The most frequently cited reasons for seeking to die stemmed from loss of enjoyable activities, loss of autonomy, and loss of dignity. Yet these were mentally alert individuals who should have been aided by professionals and their own social networks to discern that autonomy and dignity can reside in self-expression, in determining what activities to pursue, and in obtaining the assistance to undertake them. This reframing of autonomy and dignity is urgently necessary as a way to restore self-respect and pride to people who feel shame at needing physical or emotional help from those around them. Have they lost their own ability to provide love, support, friendship, and guidance to their families and friends, and if so, what professional psychological help might let them regain those capacities? Or have they lost their connections to the social world, and so been denied a way to give and to receive help and support?

For people living with disabilities, the data on Oregon's assisted suicides provokes concern. One can respect individual choice but worry that the Oregon data, like the case involving ventilator withdrawal, graphically support Burt's reflections on the ambivalence of health care professionals and families toward people with significant disability. When these data reveal that fear of burdening others is of much greater concern to patients who seek suicide than concerns about finances or physical pain, then how can professionals and families know that the supposedly autonomous wish to end life is not a response to a patient's deep fear that she has become disliked, distasteful to, and resented by the very people from whom she seeks expertise, physical help, and emotional support? And when we learn that divorced and never-married individuals are twice as likely as married or widowed people to use physician-assisted suicide, we must ponder whether a single dying person feels especially alone and abandoned. It is probably the rare friend who has the time, energy, or willingness to make a sustained, reliable, and deep commitment to live through another's illness and death. Once the severely disabled, ill, or dying person is seen as "other"—as different, not quite in the human and moral community, even past friendship and familial bonds—social bonds can diminish. To anyone with the capacity to perceive the difference between warmth, toleration, and coldness in how he or she is treated by others, the thought of days, months, or years of life subject to resentful, duty-filled physical ministrations may be a fate worse than death, akin to imprisonment and solitary confinement. What needs to change is not the patient's physical or cognitive situation, but the emotional and interpersonal environment; that environment can change only when professionals lead the way to supporting the capacities and thereby affirming the humanity of severely ill and imminently dying people. . . .

The disability equality perspective on end of life ... cases described here should demonstrate that the alliance of disability studies and disability rights with the evangelical religious groups is more apparent than real. Disability critics of much health care practice share more with end of life reformers who seek to promote an emphasis on respect for the dignity and capacities of people facing illness, disability, and death. Like these reformers, they seek the means for maintaining dignity and capacity; the aptly named Not Dead Yet strives to convince people with disabilities, their families, and their health care providers that people can still find satisfaction and quality in their lives. The president of Not Dead Yet clearly articulated the ways in which disability opposition to life-ending decisions is truly a quest for quality, rather than sanctity, of life:

> The far right wants to kill us slowly and painfully by cutting the things we need to live, health care, public housing and transportation, etc. The far left wants to kill us quickly and call it compassion, while also saving money for others perhaps deemed more worthy.

Legalized Physician-Assisted Suicide Empowers Doctors, Not Patients

Sheldon Richman

Sheldon Richman is a senior fellow at the Future of Freedom Foundation, author of several books, and editor of the Freeman *magazine.*

Freedom is so little understood in this "land of the free" that it is often confused with its opposite. Case in point: Oregon's 1994 Death With Dignity Act. . . .

The law permits what has come to be known as physician-assisted suicide. It and the appellate ruling have been hailed as victories for patient autonomy and the right to commit suicide. Indeed, the *New York Times*, in praising the ruling, editorialized: "The voters of Oregon acted with great humanity when they decided to allow terminally ill people to determine when they have suffered enough."

But did the voters really do that? A closer look at the law shows they did not.

In fact the law lets a patient who is expected to die within six months *ask* his doctor for lethal drugs. The doctor can say no, as he has every right to do. But since a patient cannot end his own life without the doctor's consent, the law is no milestone on the road to individual freedom.

What happens when a patient makes such a request of his doctor? The state's requirements are *"stringent,"* according to Dr. Peter Goodwin, a long-time family physician and an emeritus associate professor in the Department of Family Medicine at Oregon Health and Science University. They include, Goodwin writes, "the attending physician's diagnosis/prognosis and determination that the patient is informed, capable and acting voluntarily."

Law Does Not Provide Patient Autonomy

Note that the attending physician must be convinced that the patient knows what he's doing. Whether or not you think doctors have a special ability to see the absence of volition in an action (I don't), this requirement is hardly consistent with "allow[ing] terminally ill people to determine when they have suffered enough."

But there's more. The law states, "A consulting physician must examine the patient and the medical records and concur with the attending physician's diagnosis/prognosis and assessment of the patient."

Why empower doctors? Suicide isn't a medical issue. It's a moral issue.

Dr. Goodwin comments: "If the attending physician or the consulting physician thinks the patient may suffer from a psychological disorder causing impaired judgment, the physician must refer the patient for evaluation and counseling. No medication may be prescribed unless it is *certain* the patient's judgment is not impaired" (emphasis added).

Although these requirements are called "stringent", they are actually elastic and stacked against the patient. What terminally ill patient in great pain could not be said to have impaired judgment? What's the difference between a judgment that's impaired and one that clashes with the doctor's? In a conflict between a patient who sees no better future and wants to die and a physician (perhaps supported by the patient's family) who sees the future differently, who will prevail? The doctor, of course. Yet the law is considered a blow for patient autonomy. How can there be "death with dignity" when the patient must humbly petition the doctors, then meekly wait for a unanimous ruling? . . .

Physician-assisted suicide is a fraud. As Dr. Thomas Szasz writes in his book *Fatal Freedom: The Ethics and Politics of Suicide*, "The term 'physician-assisted suicide' [PAS] is intrinsically mendacious [dishonest]. The physician is the principal, not the assistant. In the normal use of the English language, the person who assists another is the subordinate; the person whom he assists is his superior. . . . However, the physician engaging in PAS is superior to the patient: He determines who qualifies for the 'treatment' and prescribes the drug for it."

In other words, the Oregon law has nothing to do with the freedom of the individual and everything to do with the power of doctors. If freedom were the concern, we would simply repeal the drug and prescription laws, and recognize each adult's right to buy any kind of drugs.

Why empower doctors? Suicide isn't a medical issue. It's a moral issue.

CHAPTER 3

Would Assisted Suicide Be a Slippery Slope?

Chapter Preface

The main objection to legalization of assisted suicide, apart from religious grounds, is that it may be a "slippery slope" issue. According to the dictionary, a slippery slope is "a course of action that seems to lead inevitably from one action or result to another with unintended consequences." In other words, one thing leads to another, which is true in many areas of life—once a relatively small concession is granted, the door is opened to larger ones. Most people, from teenagers arguing with their parents to politicians arguing with each other, are well aware of this tendency. But the term generally is used only in connection with controversies in which both sides agree that the ultimate alleged consequences would be negative.

Would legalized assisted suicide be a slippery slope? Supporters of assisted suicide believe that it is okay for people who are in pain and will soon die anyway to take drugs that will kill them quickly. Advocates of assisted-suicide laws once claimed that dying patients were the only people who would be affected. According to statistics, however, Oregon's law has been used less by people in pain than by those who fear the loss of their independence and dignity, so physical pain is no longer viewed as the main criterion. Still, the Oregon law applies only to terminally ill patients who are mentally competent. Most supporters maintain that this always will be the case. Opponents believe that such laws will be extended to people who suffer from chronic illnesses or disabilities that are not terminal, but are costly and life debilitating--perhaps eventually even to the mentally ill. Moreover, many fear that in time not merely the prescribing of deadly drugs but also their active administration—that is, euthanasia—will be legalized, as has happened in the Netherlands.

This is not the only slippery-slope argument. Another is that if assisted suicide is legalized, sick people may be pressured into requesting it if they cannot afford medical care to relieve their suffering. Insurers, they say, may encourage assisted suicide to avoid the cost of keeping such patients alive. Disability-rights activists fear that availability of assisted suicide will sway the public into thinking that some people's lives are not worth living, and that the ill and disabled may be led to feel that they have a duty to die rather than burden society with their care.

Supporters point out that these fears have not materialized in Oregon. But even in Oregon assisted suicide is not widely viewed as an option. Older people who are now developing terminal illnesses have lived their lives during an era when no justification for suicide was socially acceptable. With time, as younger generations with different moral and cultural values age, this attitude may change as well, leading more terminally ill people to opt for assisted suicide.

Assisted-suicide advocates argue that proposed laws contain safeguards against abuse. Although such safeguards could prevent the killing of people against their will, some patients might sincerely wish to spare their loved ones the ordeal of seeing them suffer. Anglican archbishop Peter Jensen of Sydney, Australia, speaking of the death of his mother from cancer, said, "We would not have had to say anything; a hint from us plus a system in which assisted suicide was a possibility, and she would have demanded her own death." The assisted-suicide debate is not just a matter of whether or not people have a right to die. The viewpoints in the following chapter reflect the slippery-slope concerns of euthanasia, financial pressures, pain and suffering of family members, and how nonterminal patients may be affected.

Assisted Suicide Will Not Remain Restricted to the Terminally Ill

Wesley J. Smith

Wesley J. Smith is a senior fellow at the Discovery Institute, an attorney for the International Task Force on Euthanasia and Assisted Suicide, and a special consultant to the Center for Bioethics and Culture. He is the author of several books.

Should laws against assisted suicide be rescinded as "paternalistic"? Should assisted suicide be transformed from what is now a crime (in most places) into a sacred "right to die"? Should assisted suicide be redefined from a form of homicide into a legitimate "medical treatment" readily available to all persistently suffering people, including to the mentally ill?

According to Brown University professor Jacob M. Appel, the answer to all three of these questions is an unequivocal yes. Writing in the May–June 2007 *Hastings Center Report* ("A Suicide Right for the Mentally Ill?"), Appel argues that assisted suicide should not only be available to the terminally ill, but also to people with "purely psychological disease" such as victims "of repeated bouts of severe depression," if the suicidal person "rationally might prefer dignified death over future suffering."

Given the emphasis assisted suicide advocates and the media normally give to the role of terminal illness in the assisted suicide debate, it might be tempting to dismiss Appel as a fringe rider. But he most definitely is not. Over the last several years, advocacy for what is sometimes called "rational suicide" has been growing increasingly mainstream, discussed among the bioethical and academic elite in mental health publications, academic symposia, and books. Indeed, it is worth noting that Appel's essay appeared in the world's most prestigious bioethics journal.

As disturbing as Appel's proposal is—it is essentially a call for death-on-demand—it is refreshing that Appel has written so candidly. After years of focus group–tested blather from the political wing of the euthanasia movement claiming that legalizing assisted suicide would be strictly limited to the terminally ill, we finally have a clearer picture of where the right-to-die crowd wishes to take America.

Assisted suicides for the mentally ill are already taking place in euthanasia-friendly locales.

Moreover, unlike a restricted right to assisted suicide, Appel's call for near death-on-demand is logically consistent. There are two weight-bearing intellectual pillars that support euthanasia and assisted suicide advocacy: (1) a commitment to a radical individualism that includes the right to choose "the time, manner, and method of death" (often called "the ultimate civil right" by assisted suicide aficionados); and (2) the fundamental assumption that killing is an acceptable answer to the problems of human suffering. Appel describes these conjoined beliefs succinctly as the "twin goals of maximizing individual autonomy and minimizing human suffering" by avoiding "unwanted distress, both physical and psychological" through creation of a legal right "to control . . . when to end their own lives."

Assisted Suicide for the Mentally Ill

Hoping to whistle past the graveyard, some might dismiss all of this as mere theoretical posturing. Were it so. Assisted suicides for the mentally ill are already taking place in euthanasia-friendly locales. Indeed, nearly every jurisdiction that has legalized assisted suicide for the seriously ill—as well as those that have refused to meaningfully enforce anti–assisted suicide laws—has either formally expanded the legal right to die to those suffering existentially, or shrugged in the face of illegal assisted suicides of the depressed. To wit:

Switzerland: In February [2007], the Swiss Supreme Court ruled that the mentally ill have a constitutional right to assisted suicide, because, as reported in the *International Herald Tribune*, "It must be recognized that an incurable, permanent, serious mental disorder can cause similar suffering as a physical (disorder), making life appear unbearable to the patient in the long term."

The natural trajectory of assisted suicide advocacy leads to . . . ever-widening expansions of killable categories.

The Netherlands: The Dutch Supreme Court issued a similar ruling back in 1993 when it approved a psychiatrist assisting the suicide of his chronically depressed patient who wanted to die due to unremitting grief caused by the deaths of her adult children—even though the doctor never attempted to treat the woman. The basis for the ruling followed the above described logic of euthanasia: Suffering is suffering and it doesn't matter whether the cause is physical or emotional, meaning that Dutch mercy killing need not be limited to the sick and disabled.

The United States: We saw a similar phenomenon in America's reaction to the decade-long assisted suicide campaign of Jack Kevorkian. Not only were the majority of Kevorkian's "patients" not terminally ill (most were disabled)—but several were not even sick. For example, Marjorie Wantz, Kevorkian's second assisted suicide who died on October 23, 1991, complained about severe pelvic pain. Her autopsy revealed that nothing was wrong physically. It turned out that she had been hospitalized previously for mental problems. In 1996 Rebecca Badger went to Kevorkian complaining of having multiple sclerosis. Her autopsy proved that she was disease free. It was later reported that she had been depressed and addicted to pain pills. Despite these and other such cases of his assisting the depressed to kill themselves, Kevorkian remained publicly popular until he was finally jailed in 1999 after he videotaped himself murdering Lou Gehrig's patient Thomas Youk by lethal injection.

Oregon: Advocates for legalizing assisted suicide frequently tout Oregon's law as proving that assisted suicide can be restricted to the terminally ill. In actuality, little is known about what is happening in the state because it gets information about these practices almost exclusively through self-reporting by participating doctors.

Even so, the curtain was pulled back briefly when a peer-reviewed article in the June 2005 *American Journal of Psychiatry* appeared describing a potential assisted suicide of a psychotic man that was disturbingly similar to what is happening in the Netherlands and Switzerland. After cancer patient Michael J. Freeland received a lethal prescription, he had to be hospitalized for mental illness. Despite being delusional, his psychiatrist permitted him to keep the fatal overdose, in the doctor's words, "safely at home"—even though this same doctor advised a court that Freeland would "remain vulnerable to periods of delirium" and would "be susceptible to periods of confusion and impaired judgment." (Freeland died naturally nearly two years after receiving his lethal prescription—meaning he was also not terminally ill as defined by Oregon's law when he was prescribed the lethal overdose in the first place.) Needless to say, nothing was done to remedy this apparent breach of law.

Increasing Eligibility for Assisted Suicide

The natural trajectory of assisted suicide advocacy leads to such ever-widening expansions of killable categories: from the terminally ill, to the disabled and chronically ill, to the "tired of life" elderly, and eventually to the mentally ill. Appel understands this and approves. He writes:

> Contemporary psychiatry aims to prevent suicide, yet the principles favoring legal assisted suicide lead logically to the extension of these rights to some mentally ill patients. But now that several Western nations and one U.S. state have liberalized their laws, it seems reasonable to question the policies that universally deny such basic opportunities to the mentally ill.

With the truth now clearly in view, the time has come to have real debate about the so-called right to die. This debate should not pretend that the practice will be limited and rare and it should fully address the societal implications of transforming assisted suicide into a mere medical treatment.

So, let's argue openly and frankly about the wisdom of permitting near death-on-demand as a method of ending serious and persistent suffering. Let's discuss whether "choice" and "individual autonomy" requires that we permit licensed and regulated euthanasia clinics to serve anyone who has made an irrevocable decision to die.

Indeed, let's argue whether or not society owes a duty of prevention to the self-destructive who are not acting on mere impulse. But finally, let's stop pretending that assisted suicide legalization would be just a tiny alteration in public policy restricted only to the terminally ill. That clearly isn't true.

Legalized Assisted Suicide May Lead to Legalized Euthanasia

Susan W. Enouen

Susan W. Enouen is a professional engineer who volunteers for the Life Issues Institute, a nonprofit pro-life educational organization.

In 1994, Oregon voters approved the *Death with Dignity Act* (DWDA) by a vote of 51% to 49%. It became effective in 1998, surviving court challenges and a repeal effort, to make Oregon the first state in the country to legalize physician-assisted suicide (PAS). The law allows physicians to prescribe life-ending drugs that are requested by terminally ill patients with six months or less to live. In the nine years since then, DWDA records show that 455 people have requested lethal drugs from their physician and 292 people have died from using them. The yearly numbers continue to rise, beginning with 16 deaths in 1997, increasing to 38 in 2005, and reaching 46 deaths in 2006. Although these records show that relatively few Oregonians choose to use this option, the lack of accountability and safeguards in the process have many people concerned that the numbers are not telling the whole story. In addition to that, disturbing trends appear to be developing.

For example, only 17 complications have been reported in the 292 deaths, and 16 of these were regurgitation. However, in the Netherlands, where they have had many years to work on overcoming complications in assisted suicide, serious complications are still reported. In fact, a study found that Dutch doctors feel the need to intervene (by giving lethal injections) in 18% of cases because of complications or problems. The lack of reported complications in Oregon has caused even pro-assisted suicide physicians to question the credibility of Oregon's reported data.

One of the reasons to suspect the accuracy of the data is that the prescribing physician is not required by law to be present when the drugs are taken. Since 2001, when this data was first collected, prescribing physicians had only been present at 29% of the deaths. The recording of complications is therefore dependent upon the self-report of a physician who, in most cases, was not even present, and who must rely on second-hand information or guesswork to file a report. The Oregon Department of Human Services (DHS), which collects the information, must depend on the word of the doctors for the reliability of their data and "it has no authority to investigate individual Death with Dignity cases."

What Happens to Unused Lethal Drugs?

Even more chilling is the fact that the *Death with Dignity Act* applies no penalties to doctors who do not report that they have prescribed lethal drugs for the purpose of suicide. This means that there is no way to know for sure how many assisted-suicide deaths may actually be occurring in Oregon. Nor is there any way to know whether the prescribed drugs are being made available to people other than the patient who requested them. Only 64% of patients who have received the prescriptions are known to have died from taking them. What becomes of all the other deadly drugs? It is possible the prescriptions have never been filled, or maybe the lethal drugs are sitting in medicine cabinets unused, but clearly there is the potential for accidents, and the law provides very little safeguard from abuse. So far, no one has been disciplined for disregarding the safeguards that the law does provide. Complications are not investigated and likely not reported in many cases, and the reality is DHS "has no regulatory authority or resources to ensure compliance with the law."

According to the Oregon data, the majority of patients who choose assisted suicide have some type of cancer, have a median age of about 70 years, are overwhelmingly white (98–), somewhat more likely to be male (57–), have had at least a partial college education (63–), are enrolled in hospice care (86–), and die at home (93–). The most common concerns given for choosing assisted suicide are "losing autonomy" (87–), being "less able to engage in activities making life enjoyable" (87–), and "loss of dignity" (80–). (The last category was added in 2003.) No category is provided to indicate whether or not the patient might be depressed, yet all of these concerns have much to do with a patient's gloomy appraisal of life, a possible indicator of treatable depression. Still only 4–5% of patients were referred for psychiatric evaluation from 2003 to 2006, having dropped from 37% in 1999, to 13% in 2002 and reaching its lowest point of 4% in 2006. This indicates a weakening response on the part of prescribing doctors to ensure that the patient is truly capable of making such a decision.

It is much more cost effective and easier to let people kill themselves, and it can be rationalized as a compassionate approach.

Prescriptions from Unfamiliar Doctors

There may be a reason for this trend. One of the safeguards touted by the promoters of assisted suicide was that this decision would be made between the patient and his long-time trusted doctor. This familiar doctor would discuss all other options with the patient and would be able to evaluate the patient's true physical and psychological state. To prevent hasty decisions, the law requires a patient to make two oral requests for the lethal drugs, at least two weeks apart, before the physician can prescribe them. Yet for the past 6 years, the minimum recorded duration for a patient-physician relationship has been 1 week or less. Not only does this indicate that at least some doctors are not following the law's requirements, but with a median duration of about 12 weeks, it means that most patients are not receiving these prescriptions from a trusted doctor who knows them well.

In fact, many physicians are unwilling to write lethal prescriptions, causing at least one HMO [health maintenance organization] to make an email plea to enlist doctors who would be willing to act as the "attending physician" for patients requesting assisted suicide. And nurses' organizations admit to sending patients to an assisted-suicide advocacy group when their own doctor does not want to participate. These patients then find a doctor through the advocacy group Compassion and Choices (formerly called Compassion in Dying, until it merged with the Hemlock Society in 2005), which sees "almost 90% of requesting Oregonians."

Acceptance of assisted suicide can lead to involuntary euthanasia of the disabled and dying, which can lead to legal euthanasia.

Not only are assisted-suicide patients becoming disengaged from their trusted doctors and relying heavily upon the aid of an assisted-suicide advocacy group, but HMO's are becoming involved in administering assisted suicide, a much cheaper option for them than paying for longer-term palliative care that would focus on alleviating a patient's pain.

It is much more cost effective and easier to let people kill themselves, and it can be rationalized as a compassionate approach. One of the primary arguments for assisted suicide is the ending of unbearable physical pain. Experience in The Netherlands, where euthanasia is legal, is revealing. Concern that pain will become unbearable is common, this being a worry in one-third or more of such patients. However, the Dutch experience is that of those actually requesting euthanasia, only 5% list physical pain as their major reason, and typically when pain is controlled they change their mind. As noted above, loss of autonomy and other psychologically "painful" concerns are the overwhelming majority of reasons given.

All in all, there are many troubling aspects of Oregon's assisted suicide law, and yet several states have tried to follow suit with nearly identical bills. California, Hawaii, Arizona, Vermont and Wisconsin have all faced assisted-suicide bills in their legislatures this year [2007], and for some of these states it has been an ongoing attempt for several years. As assisted-suicide proponents continue to lobby for this legislation, their language has evolved into less threatening-sounding terms. Rather than "physician assisted suicide," the phrase is "physician aid in dying" or PAD, so physicians now "induce PAD." In fact, the DHS has been threatened with litigation if the state continues to use the word "suicide." Other euphemisms include "patient choice," "control at end of life," "assisted death" and "death with dignity." This is all part of a program to help people think of it as a compassionate approach to death.

From Assisted Suicide to Euthanasia

Where will the Oregon experiment go from here? The Netherlands' experience has shown that acceptance of assisted suicide can lead to involuntary euthanasia of the disabled and dying, which can lead to legal euthanasia. This melds easily into illegal but accepted euthanasia of disabled and dying babies. It is then just a small baby step to legalize the infanticide of such "suffering" little ones. This is where the thinking in The Netherlands has gone in the past 30 years. As Wesley J. Smith, an anti-euthanasia advocate, author, and an attorney for the International Task Force on Euthanasia and Assisted Suicide, says about the euthanasia movement: "euthanasia and assisted suicide have gone . . . from the unthinkable, to the debatable, to the justifiable, on its way to unexceptional."

We would be wise to keep a very close eye on Oregon.

Use of Euphemisms Attempts to Ease Acceptance of Assisted Suicide

Rita L. Marker and Wesley J. Smith

Rita L. Marker is an attorney and executive director of the International Task Force on Euthanasia and Assisted Suicide. Wesley J. Smith is a senior fellow at the Discovery Institute, an attorney for the International Task Force on Euthanasia and Assisted Suicide, and a special consultant to the Center for Bioethics and Culture.

The Vermont legislature has fast-tracked a bill to legalize physician-assisted suicide, and California may not be far behind. If the legislatures in these states do vote to redefine physician-assisted suicide as a legitimate and legal "medical treatment," a large part of the blame, strange though it may sound, can be laid at the feet of postmodernism.

The deconstruction of language, with disregard for facts and accurate definitions, is infecting medical and health-care ethics and policies. Case in point: In order to further the legitimization of assisted suicide, the American Public Health Association (APHA) embraced the political advocacy of assisted-suicide supporters in November [2006] when it decided that "physician-assisted suicide"—an accurate and descriptive term—should be replaced with the euphemistic advocacy-phrase "aid in dying." At its annual meeting, the organization approved an interim policy:

> Urges health educators, policy-makers, journalists and health care providers to recognize that the choice of a mentally competent, terminally ill person to choose to self-administer

medications to bring about a peaceful death is not "suicide," nor is the prescribing of such medication by a physician "assisted suicide." Urges terms such as "aid-in-dying" or "patient-directed dying" be used to describe such a choice.

This policy [was to] become permanent if confirmed by the APHA's governing council in 2007.

The stakes in this semantics game are high. At issue—and indeed, the whole point of this postmodernist exercise—is whether activists will be able to convince other states to join Oregon in redefining the crime of assisted suicide as a legitimate "medical treatment." If that happens, funding of assisted suicide would soon follow, just as it has in Oregon, where the act of facilitating suicide is now deemed a state-funded form of "comfort care."

Thus far . . . the press has, for the most part, not jumped on the name-change bandwagon.

Assisted Suicide Movement Losing Support

In one sense, the opening of this new front in the assisted-suicide debate reveals that the movement, thought to be unstoppable when Oregon passed the nation's first assisted-suicide law, understands that it has failed to convince America that suicide should be part of medicine's armamentarium [range of materials or options available]. In the more than ten years since the passage of the Oregon law, state after state has considered legalizing assisted suicide. Each time, there was early support for the measure. Yet, in each instance, when the official vote was taken, support had evaporated and the proposal went down in defeat. This left assisted-suicide proponents, particularly Compassion & Choices (C & C) (formerly the Hemlock Society), which spearheaded most of these legislative proposals, searching for some way to improve their position.

So C & C commissioned research and polling. They found that people have a negative impression of the term "assisted suicide," but, if euphemistic slogans like "death with dignity" or "end of life choices" were used to describe the same action, response was relatively positive. Likewise, poll respondents were more apt to approve letting doctors "end a patient's life" than they were to approve giving doctors the right to "assist the patient to commit suicide." According to one polling firm, the apparent conflict was a "consequence of mentioning, or not mentioning, the word 'suicide.'"

As a result, assisted-suicide advocates concluded that the accurate word "suicide" had to go. They embarked on a crusade to erase and replace it with kinder, gentler language that masked the harsh reality of what was being discussed.

Their line of attack aimed at three target groups: the media, the state of Oregon, and major public-policy organizations. If those groups could be persuaded to adopt new language, opposition would supposedly disappear.

Accordingly, they issued press releases claiming that use of the term "assisted suicide" demonstrated insensitivity to dying patients and to the physicians who assisted them. In one C & C press release, Dr. Peter Goodwin, who has presided over a number of assisted-suicide deaths, said, "As a physician, I resent the term 'physician-assisted suicide.' I never felt I was assisting a suicidal patient, but rather aiding a patient with his or her end of life choice."

Thus far, however, the press has, for the most part, not jumped on the name-change bandwagon. For example, the Associated Press bureau chief in Portland, Oregon, said, "We have thought about it and we feel 'suicide' describes the act of taking one's life, so we'll stick with it—for the time being." Likewise, the *Register-Guard* (Eugene, Oregon) will continue to use the terms "doctor- or physician-assisted suicide," since they have chosen "to err on the side of plain English."

Oregon Adopts New Terminology

The government of Oregon, however, is another story. The Oregon Department of Human Services (DHS) is the entity charged with compiling annual assisted-suicide statistics, and, since those statistics are inevitably part of any debate or discussion about new assisted-suicide measures, C & C needed the DHS to replace the offending "s-word" in the reports. To accomplish this, C & C first sent a formal request to the state agency, suggesting that the terms "aid-in-dying," "directed dying," or "assisted dying" be used in official state reports. Then the group upped the ante when it brought lawyers to a meeting with the DHS to discuss the language substitution and implied that, if it were not made, litigation might follow.

Rather than risk a legal wrangle (or, perhaps, out of sympathy for the cause), the state acquiesced. On October 16, [2006] state officials announced that, in the future, physician-assisted suicides in Oregon would be listed as "physician-assisted death." However, this label was changed after a number of Oregonians objected to its ambiguity, since it could refer to anything from plumping a pillow or wiping a brow to intentionally giving an overdose of a lethal drug.

Apparently, suicide is no longer a problem if it isn't called "suicide."

The state agency finally settled on the phrase it would use instead of "physician-assisted suicide." In all future official communication, the state of Oregon will refer to patients who die from physician-assisted suicide as "persons who use the Oregon Death with Dignity Act."

Assisted-suicide activists were ecstatic. According to Kathryn Tucker, C & C's director of legal affairs, "This will be a sea change because how you speak of things strongly influences how you think of them."

The victory in Oregon was equaled when the APHA announced that it would embrace the misleading language. With over 50,000 members from over 50 occupations in the public-health field, APHA has a long arm. According to its web site, "APHA has been influencing policies and setting priorities in public health for over 125 years." Now it will give the media an excuse to shift from precise and accurate descriptive language about assisted suicide to the words of pure political advocacy. Clearly, the APHA's adoption of a policy intended to mask the reality of suicide and to legitimize its facilitation by describing it in innocuous terms constitutes thinly veiled support for passage of laws permitting physician-assisted suicide.

Advocates Use Words for Political Purposes

This is a big shift from 1999, when then-U.S. Surgeon General David Satcher declared, "Suicide is a serious public health problem," and urged implementation of a comprehensive national strategy for suicide prevention. At the time, he did not recommend that those who had been diagnosed (or misdiagnosed) with a terminal illness be exempt from efforts at suicide prevention. But Satcher himself has now caught assisted-suicide fever. In 2006 (when he was no longer the surgeon general), he wrote a letter supporting a California bill that was identical to Oregon's law. (The California bill failed.) In his letter, he referred to assisted suicide in Oregon as "legal aid in dying in Oregon." Apparently, suicide is no longer a problem if it isn't called "suicide."

Let's think about how this works: Take a patient who has been diagnosed with a terminal condition. If that patient asks her doctor for sleeping pills so she can sleep comfortably at night, and if the doctor prescribes them, but she takes all of the pills at once and dies, her death is called "suicide."

But, if that same patient asks her doctor for sleeping pills so she can die, and if the doctor prescribes them for that purpose, and she takes all of the pills as directed and dies, her death is not called "physician-assisted suicide."

Assisted-suicide advocates say that that's proper, but really it's just political correctness. By bringing postmodernism to health-care public-policy, they hope to drive their agenda to victory.

Research That Found No Slippery Slope Effect Was Invalid

Meg Jalsevac

Meg Jalsevac is a staff writer for LifeSiteNews.com, a nonprofit Web site devoted to issues of culture, life, and family.

One of the many arguments against euthanasia, widely held by activists and medical professionals alike, is the fear that legalized physician-assisted suicide will result in a "slippery slope effect" resulting in the coerced suicide of vulnerable individuals. A new study . . . published in the October [2007] issue of the *Journal of Medical Ethics* is purporting to have put that objection to rest by proving that, in areas where euthanasia has been legalized, there has been no such "slippery slope" effect.

The research was led by University of Utah professor, Margaret Battin, known as an expert in the 'ethics' of suicide and a prominent supporter of physician-assisted suicide. Battin's curriculum vitae is a laundry list of works pertaining to the legalization and 'morals' of euthanasia.

According to the research team, the purpose of the study was to determine if there was a significant increase in the death of any particularly vulnerable demographic such as the elderly, minorities, children or those who suffer from a chronic illness following the advent of legalized euthanasia in both Oregon and the Netherlands.

"Would these patients be pressured, manipulated or forced to request or accept physician-assisted dying by overburdened family members, callous physicians, or institutions or insurers concerned about their own profits?"

The study results prompted Battin to explain, "Fears about the impact on vulnerable people have dominated debate about physician-assisted suicide. We find no evidence to support those fears where this practice already is legal."

Use of reported records from the Oregon Department of Human Services could not be considered valid research results for a study of this nature.

According to the research report, "Those who received physician-assisted dying . . . appeared to enjoy comparative social, economic, educational, professional and other privileges."

The only specific group that did appear to have a higher rate of death in areas of legalized euthanasia were those individuals with AIDS. Although, the researchers said that they were not surprised to find that AIDS victims were more likely to seek physician-assisted death since previous studies had earlier indicated similar results.

Opponents Question Research Methods

Euthanasia opponents are, at best, skeptical of Ms. Battin's research results. Alex Schadenberg of the Euthanasia Prevention Coalition was very critical of the research methods referring to it as "propaganda" and asserting that "[t]he way in which the study was completed would leave one to question whether [Ms. Battin's] research was done simply to prove her hypothesis."

Schadenberg emphasized that Battin's use of reported records from the Oregon Department of Human Services could not be considered valid research results for a study of this nature.

"These reports are compiled from the information from reports sent in from physicians who prescribed the assisted suicide concoction. It is unlikely that a person prescribing assisted suicide would self-report information that may be considered outside of the law. .... Since the annual reports from the Oregon Department of Human Services are only based on self-reports from assisted suicide prescribing physicians, therefore they cannot be considered an accurate source for determining the level of a slippery slope in Oregon."

Schadenberg challenged Battin's results in both Oregon and the Netherlands saying that, in order to ascertain valid information for both locales, she would have had to interview all those individuals involved in an assisted suicide situation, including friends and family.

According to Schadenberg, "The reality is that a significant level of social bias exists within our culture that views certain types of disability and physical conditions as connected to intolerable suffering. Many people have accepted this social bias as normal and thus when they experience certain diseases or types of disabilities they consider their lives as not worth living. Within a structure of social bias, it is impossible to determine the slippery slope without analyzing the personal and relation[al] attitudes that lead to a decision of assisted suicide."

As previously reported by LifeSiteNews.com, a group of doctors and lawyers published a statement warning that the Netherlands experience showed "euthanasia, once legalized, cannot be effectively controlled."

"Euthanasia, initially intended for certain groups such as patients with terminal diseases will soon be performed on other groups of patients including the elderly, incapacitated patients, patients suffering with emotional distress, the disabled, and even children and newborn babies with disabilities who cannot ask for euthanasia."

Everyday reality has proved this statement to be scarily true as doctors at Holland's Groningen Academic Hospital publicly admitted to killing sick newborns beginning as early as the year 2000.

Similarly, two nurses in Oregon received only a slap on the wrist after they effectively killed a cancer patient in their care. The hospital involved did not report the incident to police and took longer than a year to investigate the crime. Prior to the publication of the investigation, the patient's family had not known that the patient had been euthanized and will always have to question whether the nurses had acted on their own initiative in killing their relative.

Legalized Assisted Suicide Does Not Lead to Increased Suicide Among the Disadvantaged

University of Utah

This viewpoint is a press release from the University of Utah.

Contrary to arguments by critics, a University of Utah–led study found that legalizing physician-assisted suicide in Oregon and the Netherlands did not result in a disproportionate number of deaths among the elderly, poor, women, minorities, uninsured, minors, chronically ill, less educated or psychiatric patients.

Of 10 "vulnerable groups" examined in the study, only AIDS patients used doctor-assisted suicide at elevated rates.

"Fears about the impact on vulnerable people have dominated debate about physician-assisted suicide. We find no evidence to support those fears where this practice already is legal," says the study's lead author, bioethicist Margaret Battin, a University of Utah distinguished professor of philosophy and adjunct professor of internal medicine.

The study [was] published in the October 2007 issue of the *Journal of Medical Ethics*. Battin conducted the research with public health physician Agnes van der Heide, of Erasmus Medical Center, Rotterdam [the Netherlands]; psychiatrist Linda Ganzini at Oregon Health & Science University, Portland; and physician Gerrit van der Wal and health scientist Bregje Onwuteaka-Philipsen, of the VU University Medical Center, Amsterdam [the Netherlands]. Van der Wal currently is inspector general of The Netherlands Health Care Inspectorate, which advises that nation's health minister.

University of Utah, "Doctor-Aided-Suicide: No Slippery Slope," University of Utah News Release, September 26, 2007. Reproduced by permission.

The research deals with the so-called "slippery slope" argument that has been made by critics of doctor-assisted suicide and has raised concern even among proponents. The argument is that by making it legal for medical doctors to help certain patients end their lives, vulnerable people will die in disproportionately large numbers.

"Would these patients be pressured, manipulated or forced to request or accept physician-assisted dying by overburdened family members, callous physicians, or institutions or insurers concerned about their own profits?" the researchers asked.

The American College of Physicians said in 2005 that it was "concerned with the risks that legalization [of physician-assisted suicide] posed to vulnerable populations, including poor persons, patients with dementia, disabled persons, those from minority groups that have experienced discrimination, those confronting costly chronic illnesses, or very young children."

Tracking Down the Data

Battin and her colleagues wanted to look at what actually has happened in two places where it is legal for doctors to help patients end their lives:

- Oregon is the only U.S. state where physician-assisted dying is legal. The Oregon Death with Dignity Act was passed by voters in 1994 and 1997, survived numerous challenges and was upheld by the U.S. Supreme Court in 2006. The law allows doctors to prescribe lethal medications to patients who have been diagnosed by two physicians as having a terminal illness and less than six months to live.

In the first nine years after the law took effect, 456 patients received lethal prescriptions and 292 of those actually used the drugs to kill themselves. That is 0.15 percent of all deaths in Oregon during the same period.

- The Netherlands has a 2002 law that allows doctors to prescribe medication for suicide or perform "voluntary active euthanasia," in which the physician rather than the patient administers life-ending medication. Dutch law does not require terminal illness, but "you have to be facing intolerable suffering," Battin says. Physician-assisted suicide and voluntary active euthanasia have been openly tolerated in the Netherlands since the 1980s under guidelines from the courts and medical groups.

Of 136,000 deaths annually in the Netherlands, about 1.7 percent are by voluntary active euthanasia, 0.1 percent by physician-assisted suicide and 0.4 percent are "extralegal" because they involve patients with no current explicit request to die, but who either made one before becoming incompetent or are perceived to be suffering intolerably.

The researchers found direct evidence that elderly people, women and uninsured people do not die in disproportionate numbers where physician-assisted death is legal.

Battin's team analyzed data on assisted suicide and voluntary active euthanasia in the Netherlands during 1985–2005— data taken from four government studies and several smaller ones. They analyzed Oregon Department of Human Services annual reports for 1998–2006, and surveys of physicians and hospice professionals.

Three Categories

The findings fell into three categories, based on the strength of the data. The researchers found:

- Direct evidence that elderly people, women and uninsured people do not die in disproportionate numbers where physician-assisted death is legal, but AIDS patients do. (The insurance data is from Oregon only; everyone is insured in the Netherlands.)

- Evidence that is partly direct and partly inferred showing that physician-assisted death does not kill disproportionate numbers of people who are poor, uneducated, racial and ethnic minorities, minors, or people with chronic physical or mental disabilities or chronic but not terminal illnesses.

- Evidence that is based on inference or that is partly contested showing that people with psychiatric illness—including depression and Alzheimer's disease—are not likely to die in lopsided numbers.

"Those who received physician-assisted dying . . . appeared to enjoy comparative social, economic, educational, professional and other privileges," the researchers write.

The researchers noted that in both Oregon and the Netherlands, people who received a doctor's help in dying averaged 70 years old, and 80 percent were cancer patients.

As for AIDS, during nine years of the Oregon Death with Dignity Act, only six patients with the disease died with physician assistance—2 percent of all deaths under the law. Yet, the researchers write, "persons with AIDS were 30 times more likely to use assisted dying" than a comparable group of non-AIDS patients who died of chronic respiratory disorders.

In a cohort of 131 homosexual men in Amsterdam who were diagnosed with AIDS between 1985 and 1992, and who died by 1995, 22 percent died via physician-assisted suicide or euthanasia. The rate may be lower now since the advent of medicines that make it possible for many patients to live with AIDS as a long-term chronic illness. . . .

"We've known for a long time from studies elsewhere that rates of assisted dying outside the law were much higher in people with AIDS," particularly in areas with large, supportive gay communities such as San Francisco, Battin says. "It's not a surprise to find high rates where physician-assisted dying is legal."

Legalizing Assisted Suicide Prevents Harm to the Vulnerable

Peter Singer

Peter Singer is an Australian philosopher. He is a professor of bioethics at Princeton University and is the author of many books in the fields of ethics and social philosophy.

The great irony of the work of right-to-life advocates who sought in vain to prolong Terri Schiavo's life is that all the publicity about the case has triggered a surge in the number of people completing advance declarations, making it clear that they do not wish to continue to live in circumstances like those in which Schiavo lived for the fifteen years before her death. Thus, the fight over the removal of Schiavo's feeding tube is likely to significantly increase the number of feeding tubes removed. More broadly, the case has revived interest in the full range of right-to-die questions, including issues like active voluntary euthanasia and physician-assisted suicide—which, because they require a patient to be competent to make decisions, raise ethical questions very different from those at issue in the Schiavo case.

When Killing Is Not Wrong

Any discussion of the ethics of voluntary euthanasia must begin by considering whether it can ever be right to kill an innocent human being. The view that this can never be right gains its strongest support from religious doctrines that claim that only humans are made in the image of God, or that only humans have an immortal soul, or that God gave us dominion over the animals—meaning that we can kill them if we wish—but reserved to himself dominion over human beings. Reject these ideas, and it is difficult to think of any morally relevant properties that separate human beings with severe brain damage or other major intellectual disabilities from nonhuman animals at a similar mental level. For why should the fact that a being is a member of our species make it worse to kill that being than it is to kill a member of another species, if the two individuals have similar intellectual abilities or if the nonhuman has superior intellectual abilities?

So, let's start again, without the preconceptions imposed on us by millennia of religious teachings, and ask: what makes it wrong to kill any being? One possible answer is: whatever goods life holds for any being, killing ends them. If happiness is good, as classical hedonistic utilitarians hold, then killing is bad, because when one is dead one is no longer happy. Or if it is the satisfaction of preferences that is good, as modern preference utilitarians hold, then killing is bad because, when one is dead, one's preferences can no longer be satisfied.

These answers suggest their own limits. First, if the future life of the being killed would hold more negative elements than positive ones—more unhappiness than happiness, more thwarting of preferences than satisfaction of them—then we have a reason for killing rather than against killing. That is, of course, relevant to the question of euthanasia. But who is to decide when a being's life contains, or is likely to contain, more positive characteristics than negative ones?

Freedom to Choose

The nineteenth-century philosopher John Stuart Mill argued that individuals are, ultimately, the best judges and guardians of their own interests. So in a famous example, he said that if you see people about to cross a bridge you know to be unsafe, you may forcibly stop them in order to inform them of the risk that the bridge may collapse under them, but, if they decide to continue, you must stand aside and let them cross, for only they know the importance to them of crossing and only they know how to balance that against the possible loss of their lives. Mill's example presupposes, of course, that we are dealing with beings who are capable of taking in information, reflecting, and choosing. So, here is the first point on which intellectual abilities are relevant. If beings are capable of making choices, we should, other things being equal, allow them to decide whether or not their lives are worth living. If they are not capable of making such choices, then someone else must make the decision for them, if that question should arise.

Anyone who values individual liberty should agree . . . that the person whose life it is should be the one to decide if that life is worth continuing.

Because I want to focus on voluntary euthanasia and physician-assisted suicide, I shall not now go into details regarding life-and-death decisions for those who are not capable of exercising choice. But to those who urge that, in the absence of choice, the decision should always be "for life"—as those who wanted Schiavo kept alive appear to believe—it is worth asking if they really want to insist on the use of every possible means of life support to draw out existence to the last possible minute. Very few people really want this, either for themselves or for those they love. The Roman Catholic Church does not insist on it, allowing for the withdrawal of what are sometimes called "extraordinary means." Yet, by allowing life to end earlier than it might, these proponents of "pro-life" attitudes are effectively deciding for those who are not capable of making such decisions, and they are deciding against life, not for it.

Anyone who values individual liberty should agree with Mill that the person whose life it is should be the one to decide if that life is worth continuing. If a person with unimpaired capacities for judgment comes to the conclusion that his or her future is so clouded that it would be better to die than to continue to live, the usual reason against killing—that it deprives the [person] being killed of the goods that life will bring—is turned into its opposite, a reason for acceding to that person's request.

The Slippery-Slope Argument

Undoubtedly, the most widely invoked secular argument against the legalization of voluntary euthanasia is the slippery-slope argument, i.e., that legalizing physician-assisted suicide or voluntary euthanasia will lead to vulnerable patients being pressured into consenting to physician-assisted suicide or voluntary euthanasia when they do not really want it. Or perhaps, as another version of the argument goes, they will simply be killed without their consent, because they are a nuisance to their families or because their health-care provider wants to save money. What evidence is there to support or oppose the slippery-slope argument when applied to voluntary euthanasia? A decade ago, this argument was largely speculative. Now, however, we can draw on evidence from several jurisdictions in which it has been possible for doctors to practice voluntary euthanasia or physician-assisted suicide without fear of prosecution. Active voluntary euthanasia has been openly practiced in the Netherlands since 1984, after a series of court decisions exonerated doctors who had been charged with assisting patients to die, and it was fully legalized by parliament in 1997. Belgium passed a similar law in 2002. Physician-assisted suicide—which allows the physician to prescribe a lethal dose of a drug, but not to give a lethal injection, has been legal in Switzerland for more than fifty years and in Oregon since 1997. . . .

According to Oregon officials, between 1997, when the law permitting physician-assisted suicide took effect, and the end of 2004, 208 patients used the act to end their lives. The number of patients using the act increased during the first six years and fell slightly in the seventh, but the numbers are still very small. There are about 30,000 deaths in Oregon annually, and only about 1 in every 800 deaths in that state results from physician-assisted suicide. There have been no reports of the law being used to coerce patients to commit suicide against their will and no reports of abuses have reached the Oregon Board of Medical Examiners, which has formal responsibility to investigate complaints. Contrary to suggestions that in the United States, physician-assisted suicide would be pushed upon those who are poor, less well-educated, and uninsured, Oregonians with a baccalaureate degree or higher were eight times more likely to make use of physician-assisted suicide than those without a high-school diploma, and all of those who have used the law to date have had some kind of health insurance. From all the available evidence, this does not appear to be a situation in which the law is being abused. Opponents of voluntary euthanasia contend that the open practice of voluntary euthanasia in the Netherlands has led to abuse. In the early days of nonprosecution of doctors who carried out voluntary euthanasia, prior to full legalization, a government-initiated study known as the Remmelink Report indicated that physicians occasionally—in roughly 1,000 cases a year, or about 0.8 percent of all deaths—terminated the lives of their patients without their consent. This was, almost invariably, when the patients were very close to death and no longer capable of giving consent. Nevertheless, the report gave some grounds for concern. What it did not, and could not, have shown, however, is that the introduction of voluntary euthanasia has led to abuse. To show this, one would need either two studies of the Netherlands, made some years apart and showing an increase in unjustified killings or a comparison between the Netherlands and a similar country in which doctors practicing voluntary euthanasia are liable to be prosecuted.

Such studies have become available since the publication of the Remmelink Report. First, there was a second Dutch survey, carried out five years after the original one. It did not show any significant increase in the amount of nonvoluntary euthanasia happening in the Netherlands and thus dispelled fears that that country was sliding down a slippery slope.

Studies in Australia and Belgium

In addition, studies have been carried out in Australia and in Belgium to ascertain whether there was more abuse in the Netherlands than in other comparable countries where euthanasia was illegal and could not be practiced openly. The Australian study found that while the rate of active voluntary euthanasia in Australia was slightly lower than that shown in the more recent Dutch study (1.8 percent as against 2.3 percent), the rate of explicit nonvoluntary euthanasia in Australia was, at 3.5 percent, much higher than the Dutch rate of 0.8 percent. Rates for other end-of-life decisions, such as withdrawing life support or giving pain relief foreseen to be life-shortening, were also higher than in the Netherlands. The Belgian study, which examined deaths in the country's northern Flemish-speaking region before voluntary euthanasia was legalized in that country, came to broadly similar conclusions. The rate of voluntary euthanasia was, at 1.3 percent of all deaths, again lower than in the Netherlands, but the proportion of patients given a lethal injection without having requested it was, at 3 percent of all deaths, similar to the Australian rate and also like it, much higher than the rate in the Netherlands. These two studies discredit assertions that the open practice of active voluntary euthanasia in the Netherlands had led to an increase in nonvoluntary euthanasia. There is no evidence to support the claim that laws against physician-assisted suicide or voluntary euthanasia prevent harm to vulnerable people. Those who still seek to paint the situation in the Netherlands in dark colors now need to explain the fact that that country's neighbor, Belgium, has chosen to follow its lead. The Belgian parliament voted, by large margins in both the upper and lower houses, to allow doctors to act on a patient's request for assistance in dying. The majority of Belgium's citizens speak Flemish, a language so close to Dutch that they have no difficulty in reading Dutch newspapers and books or watching Dutch television. If voluntary euthanasia in the Netherlands really were rife with abuses, why would the country that is better placed than all others to know what goes on in the Netherlands be keen to pass a similar law?

One way to interpret the results of the studies of euthanasia in Australia and Belgium, as compared with studies in the Netherlands, is that legalizing physician-assisted suicide or voluntary euthanasia brings the issue out into the open and thus makes it easier to scrutinize what is actually happening and to prevent harm to the vulnerable. If the burden of proof lies on those who defend a law that restricts individual liberty, then in the case of laws against physician-assisted suicide or voluntary euthanasia, that burden has not been discharged.

In jurisdictions where neither voluntary euthanasia nor physician-assisted suicide is legal, whether death comes sooner or later for terminally ill patients will often depend on whether or not they require a respirator—which most physicians will be prepared to withdraw. Or it may vary with how ready a physician is to administer life-shortening doses of a painkiller, perhaps risking being reported to the police by a zealously pro-life nurse. Whether we are concerned to maximize liberty or to reduce suffering, we should prefer that the time when death comes depends on the wishes of mentally competent patients. The Netherlands, Belgium, Switzerland, and Oregon now allow their citizens or residents to make that decision. There is no sound reason why other countries, and other parts of the United States, should not allow their citizens the same freedom.

Does Assisted Suicide Work Well Where It Is Practiced?

Overview: Legalized Assisted Suicide in Oregon

Colin Fogarty

Colin Fogarty is a reporter for Oregon Public Broadcasting.

These are Richard's last days. His younger brother Brian took a year off work to take care of Richard. Brian didn't want their last name used to protect his brother's privacy.

Richard has a degenerative lung disease and needs a machine to pump room air through a tube in his nose. Brian says the illness is irreversible and steadily eroding his brother's ability to breath.

Brian: "He will suffocate. And he knows from just talking with doctors and just common sense that that is a horrible way to die, just slowly choking."

Richard is getting hospice care. But Brian says his brother has also qualified for the Oregon Death with Dignity Act. So a doctor has prescribed lethal drugs that Richard can take to end his own life.

Brian: "Having a front row seat to your brother's slow demise and watching him suffer is a very difficult thing to witness. But to know that escape is now within our grasp offers a tremendous sense of comfort to him and to me."

Controversy Remains

[On October 27, 1997] the sponsors of the Oregon Death with Dignity Act celebrated the law taking effect after a long legal battle.

One of the chief petitioners, Barbara Lee, predicted the law would put families such as Brian and Richard's at ease.

Colin Fogarty, "Oregon's Death With Dignity Law Turns 10," *OPB News*, October 24, 2007. Copyright © 2007 OPB. Reproduced by permission.

Barbara Lee: "They will derive a lot of comfort and hope from just knowing that this is there . . . even if they never make a request, even if they never fill any prescriptions. It will still lighten the load."

Lee and other right to die advocates predicted Oregon would not be alone for long. Instead similar proposals have gone down in every other state that has considered them. But if right to die activists were overly optimistic, dire predictions by opponents of the Oregon law have also proven to be off the mark.

Critics said allowing terminally ill patients to end their own lives would disproportionately affect poor people, the uninsured, minorities, and patients who are mentally impaired. But according to a study this year [2007] by University of Utah researcher Margaret Battin there's no evidence of that.

Margaret Battin: "These very vivid fear mongering claims appear to be without support."

Even so the law has been under almost constant legal attack. Congress debated a change to the federal Controlled Substances Act, to prevent doctors from prescribing lethal drugs for assisted suicide.

In October 1999 Oregon Democrat [U.S. representative] Peter DeFazio railed on his Republican colleagues for trying to block a law approved twice at the Oregon ballot.

Peter DeFazio: "These people on this side of the aisle [Republicans] who are in favor of states' rights every day of the week are standing up and saying, we're for states' rights, as long as we agree with the state . . . preempting the will of the people of Oregon. It's not the state of Oregon. It's the people of the state of Oregon twice by initiative and referendum who passed this law."

The bill never passed under President [Bill] Clinton. But in 2000, then Texas Governor George W. Bush supported the change to the Controlled Substances Act.

George W. Bush: "And to the extent that controlled substances relieve pain, that's fine. But to the extent that controlled substances take a person's life, it's not fine and I would sign that bill."

Law Is Unlikely to Be Changed

But President Bush didn't have to sign a bill. Former U.S. Attorney General John Ashcroft issued a policy directive in 2001 that said physician assisted suicide is not a legitimate medical practice.

In 2006, the U.S. Supreme Court said Ashcroft overstepped his authority—a ruling that kept the Oregon law in place. Now, even the law's most vocal opponent in Oregon—Dr. Ken Stevens with the group Physicians for Compassionate Care—says the best he can hope for is to keep the law from spreading beyond Oregon.

Ken Stevens: "If anything ever changes in Oregon, it will not be in our generation. Oregonians are so independent and we have no plans to try to change it."

For Brian and his brother Richard, the most difficult questions these days are practical ones. What will be Richard's last meal? Who will he invite to his death? Brian says picking up that prescription of lethal drugs at the pharmacy made him think not about the legal, ethical, and political debate over Oregon's one of a kind law. He sat in his car weeping simply over losing his brother.

Brian: "It's a very peculiar concept. This is going to be some potion that is going to do what we've talked about doing for a long time. And now we were looking down a tunnel that was ultimately his death. And that was very sad."

Legalized Assisted Suicide Results in a Peaceful Death

Don Colburn

Don Colburn is a reporter for the Oregonian, *the leading daily newspaper of the city of Portland, Oregon.*

Lovelle Svart woke up Friday knowing it was the day she would die.

There was much to do. Her family and closest friends would be gathering at 11 AM in her mother's apartment in the Southwest Portland [Oregon] assisted-living center where they both lived.

She directed trips to the grocery store and even called AAA [American Automobile Association] to jump-start the dead battery of her 2006 Scion. She double-checked delivery of food platters from Fred Meyer [grocery store]: turkey sandwiches, strawberries and grapes, pretzels, almonds and sparkling water. There would be pink roses on the dining table and a boombox in the corner to play music, including the polka tunes she loved.

Lovelle made one last trip to "the bridge," a wooden footbridge in a nearby park where she had found quiet sanctuary the past few weeks as painful cancerous tumors spread from her lungs through her chest and her throat.

A Planned Death

The consummate planner, she had choreographed the day. She wanted to leave time—five or so hours—for storytelling, polka dancing and private goodbyes. And at 4 PM, she intended to drink a fatal dose of medication, allowed by Oregon law, that would end her life.

A smoker since age 19, Lovelle found out [in 2002] that she had inoperable lung cancer. Radiation and chemotherapy slowed the cancer's spread but could not stop it.

In June [2007], Lovelle's doctor warned her that she was likely to die within six months, making her eligible for Oregon's unique, 10-year-old Death With Dignity Act.

What some call doctor-assisted suicide and others call physician aid-in-dying or hastened death is one of the most passionately argued issues in U.S. medicine and politics. Proponents frame the question in terms of personal choice, death with dignity and freedom from pain. Opponents say assisted suicide violates the Hippocratic tradition [the doctors' code of ethics] of "First, do no harm" and undermines the doctor-patient relationship by turning physicians from healers into accomplices of death.

Lovelle . . . "touched a chord" by chronicling her "deeply intimate struggle with mortality."

Far more people ask for a lethal prescription than actually use the drug. Either their symptoms overwhelm them before they make a final decision, or they find other ways to control those symptoms, including pain.

Lovelle was determined to keep control, if possible, of when and how she died.

On July 1, she filled out and signed a one-page form titled, "*REQUEST FOR MEDICATION TO END MY LIFE IN A HUMANE AND DIGNIFIED MANNER.*" By signing, she agreed that she knew the expected result—death—and was aware of alternatives, such as hospice care.

By law, she also had to make two oral requests at least 15 days apart. Her doctor wrote the prescription for a lethal dose of barbiturate in late July, and she had it filled Aug. 7. She kept the orange bottle of clear liquid in a plastic grocery bag on a stack of towels in her bedroom closet—"hidden in plain sight," as she put it.

She was still unsure whether she would take the drug, but said she took comfort in knowing it was there.

Once she knew she had less than six months to live, Lovelle also decided to try to start a more open public discussion of dying. During the past three months, mostly through a series of online video diaries for the *Oregonian*, she shared publicly the experience of facing death.

Lovelle, 62, has "touched a chord" by chronicling her "deeply intimate struggle with mortality," said Dr. Susan Tolle, director of the Center for Ethics in Health Care at Oregon Health & Science University.

"People are following closely," Tolle said Friday. "They want to know what happens to her.

"Lovelle has become their friend."

Lovelle's three siblings and her mother, despite deep misgivings about her decision to end her life, supported Lovelle in her choice.

Her Last Day

Friday morning, Lovelle stuck a yellow note on the door of her mother's apartment: "Please Do NOT Disturb. Unless Urgent. Thank you."

She wore a blue sweat suit over a "Cancer Fighter" T-shirt.

Lovelle delighted in Friday's blustery weather and a forecast that included possible thunder and lightning about the time she planned to die. "Oh, the woo-woo crowd will have a blast with that," she said.

After AAA jump-started her car, she left the engine running to recharge the battery, returned to her apartment and set the kitchen timer for 10 minutes to remind her.

When a friend later expressed shock that Lovelle had spent part of the last morning of her life dealing with a dead car battery, Lovelle explained:

"The car goes to my sister. I didn't want it to be dead."

In the living room, her family and friends sat and told stories and jokes, sometimes with political references. At times they laughed a bit too loudly, out of nervousness at the occasion. Twice, Lovelle came out of the bedroom where she was having private meetings to say, "No politics!"

A bit later, Lovelle and George Eighmey, head of Compassion & Choices of Oregon, an advocacy group that works with most of the Oregonians who end their lives under the Death With Dignity Act, danced a brief but rousing polka.

By midafternoon, the studiously punctual Lovelle was falling behind her schedule. No one complained.

But a little before 4 PM, she decided it was time to make her final preparations. First, she had to take the two premedication pills—to calm her stomach and control vomiting. They were hard to swallow, given the tumors in her neck, but she got them down with water.

"It" would be in about an hour, she told her family. Time now to sit alone with her mom, Vi Svart, in her bedroom for the last time. The rest of the group sat in the living room, debating whether they wanted—and whether Lovelle wanted them—to be in the room with her at the end.

Lovelle's three siblings and her mother, despite deep misgivings about her decision to end her life, supported Lovelle in her choice.

"I feel so at peace," Lovelle said. "I've had such a good time. . . . And today has been so wonderful.

"I'm really ready to go. I'm ready."

About 4:30, Lovelle announced she wanted "a hugging line"—one last hug for everybody. "You'll be first and last," she said, turning to her mom.

Lovelle stood in the center of the living room and embraced them one by one—long hugs with tears and laughter.

Then one last cigarette break on her favorite sitting stone next to the parking lot. Afterward, Lovelle took the elevator up to the third-floor apartment and hung up her coat and hat.

"OK," she said to no one in particular. "I'm going to get into bed now."

In many ways, Lovelle fits the pattern of Oregonians who choose to end their lives under the Death With Dignity Act.

Like most, she had cancer. She was in her 60s. Well educated and insured. Not formally religious. White. Enrolled in hospice care.

And fiercely independent.

"I could be very gregarious—and very private," she said. "Very much the partygoer—and very much want to stay home and read."

She was chosen Miss Cafeteria at Crater Lake Lodge in the summer of 1963, and she has the lemon-yellow rayon dress to prove it. She left it hanging in a plastic dry-cleaning bag on her bathroom door.

She loved surfboarding and polka-dancing and both her first and last names, "because they are different, and I like things that are different."

And she liked, as she was the first to admit, being in control.

Final Freedom

Lovelle decided it was more important to die by taking the lethal drug while she had a degree of control over her body than to wait for nature to take its course. But how to decide when?

Her symptoms—shortness of breath, stomach distress, weakness and pain—were intensifying. If she waited too long, she would be unable to drink and swallow the lethal drug on her cupboard shelf.

Lovelle sought a shifty window between life-worth-living and incapacity, "this tiny bit of freedom" when, for her last act, she could swallow a fatal potion in the company of family and friends. "That's when I want to go."

Last Sunday, after a painful, restless night, Lovelle decided it was almost time.

Swallowing was more painful than ever, like choking on broken glass or razor blades, she said. She had barely eaten in two weeks. She started taking morphine to dull her pain.

She told family and friends to come Friday.

Lovelle sat on the foot of the bed, while 10 others gathered around. A photograph of Lovelle as a curly-haired 5-year-old stood on one bedside table; on the other were a glass tumbler containing the liquid medication, which looked like water, along with a container of morphine and Lovelle's ever-present mug of Gatorade. On the wall above the head of the bed were five more family photographs.

With some help, Lovelle yanked off her shoes and socks and slipped partway under the covers.

Eighmey stood by her bedside. He has attended more than three dozen deaths of this kind.

"Is this what you really want?"

"Actually, I'd like to go on partying," Lovelle replied, laughing before turning serious. "But yes."

"If you do take it, you will die."

"Yes."

Ever the detail person, she reminded him that she wanted her glasses and watch removed, "after I fall asleep."

Eighmey warned her that the clear liquid would taste bitter. She needn't gulp it. She would have about a minute and a half to get it down.

Lovelle dipped her right pinky into the glass and tasted. "Yuck," she said. "That's why I need the Gatorade."

Holding the glass, Eighmey asked her again to affirm that this was her wish.

Yes, she replied.

Someone asked, "Can we have another hugging line?"

One by one, they came to head of the bed for hugs and teary whispers.

"Sweet dreams."

"It's all right."

"I know."

"Thank you for being my big sister."

"All the church is praying for you."

Lovelle was sitting up in bed, three pillows propping her up.

She held the glass tumbler in her right hand, raised it to her lips and drank. It was 8 minutes after 5.

"Most godawful stuff I ever tasted in my life," she said, making a face before taking a sip of Gatorade and plain water.

She lay back and scrunched down under the covers, glasses still on to see her loved ones.

She reached for her mother, who leaned closer, then lay down next to Lovelle, stroking her hand.

"Are you OK, honey?"

"I'm fine, Mom."

"You're not sick?"

"No. I'm peaceful. It stopped raining, the sun's out. And I've had a wonderful day."

Her eyes closed.

"It's starting to hit me now."

Bedside Vigil

For a while, no one moved or spoke, as Lovelle drifted into a coma. Then Lovelle's mom asked for a prayer. Others spoke up with prayers and memories, which prompted other stories. Lovelle's brother Larry read part of [poet] William Wordsworth's "Intimations of Immortality."

Lovelle lay motionless but for the gentle rise and fall of her chest. Her heart slowed but didn't stop.

About an hour into the vigil, Lovelle's mom lit three white candles in cut-glass candlesticks in the living room. "She's still with us," she said.

Hours passed. Given what Lovelle's body had been through—not only lung cancer but also open-heart surgery in 2004, Eighmey was surprised how long she was lingering. But not her family.

"I hate to say this," one said with a smile, "but this is just like her."

"A little spitfire," agreed another.

"Above average—that's Lovelle."

"One last reminder that she's the one in control."

Jane O'Dell, a volunteer for Compassion & Choices, sat at Lovelle's bedside all evening, holding her right hand, whispering to her, monitoring her breathing and regularly checking the pulse in her wrist and neck.

About 10:30 PM, more than five hours after she had taken the drug, O'Dell signaled that Lovelle's breathing had become shallower and more labored. Her pulse dropped, her skin turned pallid and her fingernails bluish. It was more than a minute between breaths.

Family and friends resumed their bedside vigil, and silence again fell over the dark room. Lovelle's chest stopped moving.

Eighmey leaned over at 10:42 PM and put his ear to her chest to listen for a heartbeat. He stepped back, shaking his head and spoke in a quiet voice.

"She's gone."

People Consider Assisted Suicide for Both Physical and Psychological Reasons

Dean Blevins, Thomas A. Preston, and James L. Werth Jr.

Dean Blevins is a research health scientist for the Central Arkansas Veterans Healthcare System. Thomas A. Preston is a retired cardiologist who, at the time this paper was written, was a professor of medicine at the University of Washington in Seattle. James L. Werth Jr. is a professor of psychology at the University of Akron in Ohio.

To a large degree, the results of the studies on people who have received assisted death in Oregon have been consistent with each other and with research conducted in other states and other countries. Demographic characteristics common to those who choose PAD [physician-assisted death] (especially in Oregon and Washington) include being European American, unmarried, more highly educated, and less religious/spiritual. A consistent finding across studies is that pain and other physical symptoms are not the primary determinants of the desire to hasten death, nor are clinical depression and hopelessness. Rather, other psychosocial issues such as desire for (and fear of losing) control and self-determination, fear of experiencing an "undignified" dying process, and a desire to not be a burden on others are reported as the main reasons people choose to take medication to hasten death.

Those who choose PAD may do so based on life-long beliefs and values, which can be embedded in a person's spiritual and/or religious views, personality or patterns of coping

Dean Blevins, Thomas A. Preston, and James L. Werth Jr., "Characteristics of Persons Approving of Physician-Assisted Death," *Death Studies*, 2005, pp. 601–623. Reproduced by permission of Taylor & Francis, Ltd., http//:www.tandf.co.uk/journals, conveyed through Copyright Clearance Center, Inc., and the authors.

with stressful events, and sociopolitical or cultural views. This is consistent with the clinical lore that "people die the way they live."

Studies involving people who actually died as a consequence of PAD have yielded consistent findings; however, they conflict with results of investigations asking individuals to speculate about whether they would want assisted death in the future and, if so, why. Studies asking chronically or terminally ill individuals hypothetical questions about the potential desire for assisted death have commonly found that the desire for PAD is correlated with clinical depression and/or hopelessness. This has led to significant concern about whether individuals asking to die under the Death with Dignity Act, or requesting assisted death outside of Oregon, are doing so as a result of a psychological condition that, if alleviated, would eliminate their desire for a hastened death. Although there appear to be reasons to justify such concern, a review of the evidence suggests that appropriate screening can screen out people with ameliorable conditions such as some forms of clinical depression. . . .

The existing literature suggests that (a) individuals who say they may want assisted death in hypothetical scenarios are more likely to have a measurable amount of clinical depression and/or hopelessness than persons who actually have their deaths assisted; (b) alleviation of mild to moderate depression may not alter preferences for life-sustaining treatments; (c) persons who have died as a result of assisted death do not appear to have been clinically depressed or to have made their decision based on hopelessness; rather, (d) they appear to have based their decision on long-standing values that include a desire for control as well as concern about their own dignity and their loved ones' well-being, but no studies have directly examined the existence of such beliefs prior to requests for PAD.

Purpose of the Present Study

To date, investigators have not compared individuals' psychological status and attitudes about assisted death before and after they have become chronically or terminally ill. Such a comparison could help reconcile the apparently contradictory findings that although terminally ill individuals who respond to hypothetical scenarios by saying that they might want assisted death appear to be somewhat depressed and/or hopeless, those who actually die as a result of assisted death do not appear to be experiencing significant depression or hopelessness.

The [survey] participants [who support the availability of physician-assisted death] . . . reported that they were very satisfied with how they had lived their lives, felt very worthwhile, felt fairly little guilt or remorse, and rarely endorsed depression.

The study reported here was designed to examine the usefulness of such a study. Practical constraints prevented using a prospective design, as a very large sample of individuals would need to be followed over a long period of time to accumulate a large enough sample of individuals who requested assisted death. A reasonable alternative, given these constraints, would be to conduct a pilot study of individuals who strongly support PAD prior to the onset of a terminal illness, as, logically, members of this group would be the most likely to continue to support and even desire hastened death after the diagnosis of a terminal illness, although this has not yet been demonstrated in the literature. Thus, as a preliminary investigation of this area, we asked members of two "right-to-die" organizations committed to legalizing PAD to complete a survey consisting of questions about depression, hope, and values. Considering the lack of research in this specific area, we attempted to increase the comparability of this group to those who have chosen PAD by restricting eligibility to individuals who are both pro-assisted death (mirroring the high level of support for assisted death among Oregon completers) and believe they would request an assisted death for themselves (reflecting the intent to act on beliefs) if they were terminally ill. These selection criteria would logically create a group of research participants who would be most likely to actually ask for PAD.

The study sought to address three research questions. First, what are the key personal characteristics of persons who support PAD? Second, how do these individuals expect physical and psychosocial issues would affect their decision-making if they became terminally ill? Finally, how do current beliefs and attitudes relate to expected attitudes and mood states if confronted with a terminal illness? . . .

Recruitment Procedures

A recruitment letter . . . was printed on the letterhead of the local chapters of either the Hemlock Society or Compassion in Dying and mailed out by those agencies. . . . Each agency was asked to screen out and not send a survey to any individual who was critically or terminally ill. These organizations identified a total of 124 members in the study area (Seattle, WA) who were active as volunteers, officers, committee members, or employees. . . .

We have complete data on all 124 persons who received a survey. All but one were European American, the other was Asian American. Seventy-one (57%) were women and 53 (43%) were men. The age distribution is as follows: 8 (7%) were under 40, 37 (30%) were 40–49, 27 (22%) were 50–59, 41 (33%) were 60–69, and 11 (9%) were 70–82. Although we cannot necessarily generalize from our respondents, it is noteworthy that the demographic pattern of our participants is consistent with those who died under the Oregon Death with Dignity Act. . . .

Results of the Study

The overall results of this study provide some illumination on the characteristics of individuals who, prior to being diagnosed with a terminal illness, support the availability of PAD for others and say they would consider choosing assisted death for themselves. The findings fill a gap in the existing literature by providing data on the self-reported values, beliefs, and psychological state of advocates for assisted death. These results can advance the discussion of who is interested in, and may be more likely to request, assisted death.

Regarding their current beliefs/experiences, the participants, in general, reported that they were very satisfied with how they had lived their lives, felt very worthwhile, felt fairly little guilt or remorse, and rarely endorsed depression. The vast majority said they had never seriously considered suicide; however, as a result of our method of sample selection, all supported assisted death. They described themselves as fairly nonreligious. This is contrary to the general population, of whom only 9% report not subscribing to a particular religion. Beyond considering just formalized religion, nearly half (45%) stated that they did not believe in an afterlife. Although 21% believed in an afterlife and 28% were "not sure," none believed they would be punished in an afterlife for assisted death at the end of life, including those who believed their status would be judged by their God.

The major issues that [survey participants] . . . thought would contribute to their desire for assisted death were severe pain and severe breathlessness.

When asked to imagine they were dying, the participants thought they would be somewhat depressed, although over half (55%) said they would be sad but accepting and nearly all the rest (43%) said they would not be sad. If unable to perform activities of daily living, most participants (82%) said they would feel a loss of control and be unhappy because of being physically helpless, although they believed they would have significant support. They also said they would not want to continue living, would be concerned about burdening their loved ones, and would be concerned about the final memories their families would have of them. Nearly 90% said they find no intrinsic or spiritual value in suffering and 90% would value quality of life over the sanctity of life. The major issues that they thought would contribute to their desire for assisted death were severe pain and severe breathlessness; in addition, feeling physically helpless and being a burden to others were deemed very important. These findings are consistent with the majority of the extant literature in that they suggest that both physical and psychosocial issues are important to the desire for the option for hastened death. The results demonstrating that two physical symptoms (i.e., pain and breathlessness) were ranked as highly as psychosocial concerns is often the case in studies that ask participants to project what they would feel if dying, as opposed to asking persons with terminal illnesses themselves—who often report psychosocial issues to be of greater concern.

Suppression or expression of feelings of sadness or hopelessness may be colored by the meaning an individual gives to death.

In the hypothetical scenario, participants were approximately evenly split in whether they thought they would want treatment for depression, with about one third each saying yes, no, and unsure. If a physician said she or he thought they were depressed, 40% were unsure how they would respond and another 22% would be angry at the physician, whereas only a quarter thought they would accept the diagnosis. On the other hand, if respondents felt depressed on their own, a vast majority said they would tell someone about it. Further

159

exploration of this issue is necessary to understand the participants' reports of their anticipated reactions because it may be very important to understanding who does and does not seek necessary treatment when clinical depression manifests during terminal illness.

These data also suggest that the most important characteristic leading patients to approve of and potentially seek PAD may be the absence of beliefs that inhibit or proscribe PAD for others. Notably, the PAD subscribers did not find intrinsic value in suffering, preferred quality of life to sanctity of life, and did not fear the wrath of God, loss of salvation, or eternal damnation in afterlife—principles that would likely avert any consideration of PAD in believers. The absence of belief of punishment in afterlife for hastening death if already terminally ill appears to be more powerfully predictive than religiosity, as it was endorsed by all of the participants in the present study.

Role of Values and Beliefs

The nature and extent of existential suffering near the end of life may vary considerably according to individuals' values and beliefs. Suppression or expression of feelings of sadness or hopelessness may be colored by the meaning an individual gives to death. A person who accepts impending death as "God's will" may not suffer existentially as might the patient for whom God's will is not a meaningful factor. This was demonstrated in a [previous] study . . . where depression was more highly correlated with desire for hastened death among persons who were low in spiritual well-being. On the other hand, individuals who do not fear what may happen after they die may be less likely to be depressed and anxious as death approaches. Our study did not investigate these issues directly, so we hope future researchers will explore these dynamics further. The results of our study, however, do allow for the construction of a generalized character portrait of PAD supporters: They do not want to be a burden to others, they desire to control their own dying process, and they hold values allowing choice of how they die without fear of retribution or punishment in afterlife.

The associations between depression, anticipated depression, and past considerations of suicide among this group of PAD supporters suggest the need to consider pre-existing beliefs and attitudes among those who may be requesting assisted death, over and above possible mood disorders. Neither current nor anticipated depression were related to past considerations of suicide. Our data do not allow us to determine whether depression was a factor in any prior suicidality, which would be an important factor to consider among persons requesting assisted death. Similarly, it was not possible to examine any potential associations between depression and one's willingness to consider PAD if terminally ill; however, taking our results in concert with both of these limitations points to the need for longitudinal studies following people's mood and attitudes before and after developing a terminal illness, and comparing supporters and non-supporters of PAD, to sort out this issue. The present study provides justification for such a study. Current self-rating of depression predicts anticipated depression if terminally ill, suggesting continuity in one's mood but also a possible awareness of vulnerability to it in some situations. . . . The pattern of results across the present investigation and prior studies reinforces our interpretations regarding the importance of assessing pre-existing beliefs and prior episodes of clinical depression when working with individuals who are considering PAD, especially among pre-terminally ill supporters of assisted death.

The results related to pre-existing beliefs are important because they demonstrate that decisions to request and use PAD are most likely to be based on a long-standing value system as opposed to being an impulsive decision. Thus, particular concern should be focused on persons who appear to be acting in a way that is suddenly inconsistent with previous espoused values, that is, requesting PAD when there was never a tendency to support such action in the past. Although one can never know what one will want or will do until faced with the situation, the current data support careful assessment of sudden changes in behaviors or beliefs. . . .

This study was designed to extend previous research by examining the relationship between participant psychosocial and clinical characteristics and attitudes. Results suggest that the attitudes and beliefs of persons prior to being diagnosed with a terminal illness may be consistent with those among persons after they develop such an illness. This finding supplements the extant research and highlights the need for longitudinal studies to examine how personal characteristics relate to decision making near the end of life. These data also suggest several notable issues to be considered in any attempts to conduct such longitudinal investigations.

Europeans Increasingly Support Assisted Suicide

Donna Casey

Donna Casey is a reporter for Sun Media in Canada.

Listening to Ludwig Minelli talk about his work, it's easy to forget the 75-year-old lawyer is in the suicide tourism business.

The founder of Dignitas, the Swiss right-to-die organization, has the stark statistics at hand. There are the 753 foreigners who have visited the group's Zurich flat during the last eight years and ended their lives with an overdose of barbiturates. And there's the $6,500 service fee for clients, who go from age 20 to 95.

Assisted Suicide in Switzerland

But Minelli says his group—aided by his country's legalization of assisted suicide—wants to help those trapped in what he calls "a long, dark tunnel." "This tunnel has two exits. The first is to go to the so-called natural end with unknown pain in the future or to try to make a suicide on their own, which is very risky," explains Minelli of the dilemma bringing hundreds of despairing foreigners to his organization.

"We make an emergency exit in this tunnel and the door is wide open," says Minelli of giving citizens from far and away . . . the chance to end their suffering with a prescription overdose.

Earlier this year [2007], Elizabeth MacDonald, a 38-year-old wife and mother from Windsor, N.S. [Nova Scotia], who was crippled with multiple sclerosis, flew to Zurich with her husband Eric and ended her life at the Dignitas apartment.

In Switzerland, assisted suicides are legal as long as the agencies that help arrange the deaths do it for "honourable reasons" and don't profit from the death, aside from charging basic fees. Dignitas is one of three Swiss right-to-die groups that help arrange assisted suicides.

For many, Holland's euthanasia law is the beacon for socially progressive thinking about end-of-life care. For others, it's a symptom of a decaying and morally bankrupt society.

Minelli says Dignitas is "helping many more people to live than to help die, but the media are not very interested in living people as they are in dead people." He says roughly 70% of the clients who get the approval through Swiss law never follow through.

Clients often "discover that they have much more strength than they ever thought they had."

Assisted Suicide in Holland

For many, Holland's euthanasia law is the beacon for socially progressive thinking about end-of-life care. For others, it's a symptom of a decaying and morally bankrupt society.

University of Manitoba ethicist Dr. Arthur Schafer calls the Dutch law on physician-assisted suicide a type of "Rorschach test," with supporters and critics seeing what they want in the ink blots.

A patient age 16 or older must be "suffering unbearably" with no prospect of improvement. The request must be voluntary, well-considered and approved by two doctors. The lethal injection must be performed by a physician, who is required to report the assisted suicide to the local pathologist.

Since euthanasia was legalized in 2002, Dutch doctors face an "avalanche" of strict legal controls, says a leading legal expert on euthanasia in Europe.

For decades, doctors worked under a cloak of secrecy, reluctantly giving fatal overdoses with no accountability, says John Griffiths, professor of sociology and law at the University of Groningen in the Netherlands.

In 2005, a state committee reviewed 2,883 cases of assisted suicide to ensure all required conditions were met, including "unbearable suffering."

Today, doctors report 90% of assisted suicides and are subject to medical disciplinary rules, an independent review panel and criminal law, says Griffiths, co-author of *Euthanasia and the Law in the Netherlands.*

Opponents of the Dutch model say legalized euthanasia encourages a quick-fix solution to existential problems of aging, suffering and sickness.

Critics also say the country should improve palliative care [to ease suffering] instead of chipping away at the safeguards on euthanasia. In 2005, a review commission ruled doctors, under strict conditions, could end a patient's life even if the person isn't suffering a life-threatening illness.

Critics say the change is the start of the slippery slope, where patients can simply say they're "tired of living"—the complaint of Dutch politician Edward Brongersma, whose doctor-assisted death prompted the review of the legal criteria.

Critics also point to the "Groningen protocol," where newborns are killed, with the parents' consent, if doctors believe the baby is suffering greatly with no hope of improvement. Every year, between 15 to 20 babies born with spina bifida—a defect of brain and spinal cord deformities—are given lethal overdoses.

But Griffiths says qualifying for assisted suicide in Holland is "an uphill battle."

"Doctors hate performing euthanasia," says Griffiths, noting the overwhelming majority of people who seek death by lethal injection are elderly, well-educated men in the final stages of cancer.

Griffiths said legalizing assisted suicide has ushered in an era of "euthanasia talk." "There's now the cultural possibility to openly talk about these things," says Griffiths.

Support for Legalization in Britain

Last year [2006], an emotionally charged political debate erupted in the U.K. [United Kingdom] when an assisted-dying bill was introduced in the House of Lords.

Modelled after Oregon's Death With Dignity Act, the discussion on Lord Joel Joffe's private member's bill in May 2006 came after hundreds of submissions, thousands of letters and an unprecedented PR [public relations] campaign by the country's mainline churches.

"It just seemed to me that what this is all about is human rights and people to make decisions in relation to their own lives," says Joffe of adding another option to a country viewed as the world's leader in palliative care.

In the fevered run-up to the debate, a key question emerged—if assisted dying were legalized, would vulnerable people feel pressured to ask for help to die despite their wish to live?

Joffe says the bill was replete with protections—the patient would need to be terminally ill, living with "unbearable suffering" and required to ingest the medication by him or herself.

"It requires courage and determination by a patient to traverse the array of safeguards," says Joffe, a former human rights lawyer who once represented [political leader] Nelson Mandela in South Africa. The opposition to the bill—which was originally introduced in 2002—came in part from institutional medicine. In 2005, the British Medical Association voted to adopt a neutral stance on physician-assisted suicide, but later switched back to opposing the practice.

Joffe says the country's Christian churches used the debate to "re-establish their waning influence," unleashed a media campaign of "unprecedented ferocity."

The bill was defeated by a vote of 150–100, but Joffe feels the 40% show of support bodes well for a future attempt at changing the law, noting polls show 80% of Britons support assisted dying.

Official Data on Assisted Suicide in Oregon Are Unreliable

Rita L. Marker

Rita L. Marker is an attorney and executive director of the International Task Force on Euthanasia and Assisted Suicide.

Under Oregon's law permitting physician-assisted suicide, the Oregon Department of Human Services (DHS)—previously called the Oregon Health Division (OHD)—is required to collect information, review a sample of cases, and publish a yearly statistical report. In the first seven years during which the "Death with Dignity Act" was in effect, seven official reports were published. However, due to major flaws in the law and the state's reporting system, there is no way to know for sure how many or under what circumstances patients have died from physician-assisted suicide.

Assisted-Suicide Deaths Reported

Official reports state that there have been 208 deaths in the first seven years since the law went into effect. Those, however, are the *reported* deaths. The actual number of deaths is unknown. The latest annual report indicates that reported assisted-suicide deaths have increased by more than 225 percent since the first year of legal assisted suicide in Oregon. The numbers, however, could be far greater. From the time the law went into effect, Oregon officials in charge of formulating annual reports have conceded that there is no way to know if additional deaths went unreported because Oregon DHS has no regulatory authority or resources to ensure compliance with the law.

The DHS has to rely on the word of doctors who prescribe the lethal drugs. Referring to physicians' reports in its March 1999 CD [Current Disease] Summary, the state reporting division admitted: "For that matter the entire account [received from doctors] could have been a cock-and-bull story. We assume, however, that physicians were their usual careful and accurate selves." The Death with Dignity law contains no penalties for doctors who do not report prescribing lethal doses for the purpose of suicide.

Complications During Assisted Suicide

Official reports state that there have been ten instances of vomiting, but no other complications associated with physician-assisted suicides. Those are the *reported* complications. The actual number of complications is unknown. Prescribing doctors may not know about all complications since they are often not present when the deaths occur. During the seventh year, physicians who prescribed the lethal drugs for assisted suicide were present at fewer than 16 percent of reported deaths so the information provided by doctors may come from secondhand accounts of those present at the deaths or may be conjecture.

The fact that official reports do not reflect what is actually happening is emphasized when news accounts of complications, none of which were reflected in official reports, are taken into account.

In 1999, the *Oregonian* described the death of Patrick Matheny. Matheny received his lethal prescription from Oregon Health & Science University via Federal Express. He had difficulty when he tried to take the drugs four months later. His brother-in-law, Joe Hayes, said he had to "help" Matheny die. According to Hayes, "It doesn't go smoothly for everyone. For Pat it was a huge problem. It would have not worked without help."

169

The following year, the *Oregonian* and other Portland-area news outlets carried accounts of another case where complications occurred. Speaking at Portland Community College, pro–assisted suicide attorney Cynthia Barrett described a botched assisted suicide. "The man was at home. There was no doctor there," she said. "After he took it [the lethal dose], he began to have some physical symptoms. The symptoms were hard for his wife to handle. Well, she called 911. The guy ended up being taken by 911 to a local Portland hospital. Revived. In the middle of it. And taken to a local nursing facility. I don't know if he went back home. He died shortly—some . . . period of time after that. . . ."

Overdoses of barbiturates are known to cause vomiting as a person begins to lose consciousness. The patient then inhales the vomit. In other cases, panic, feelings of terror and assaultive behavior can occur from the drug-induced confusion. But Barrett would not say exactly which symptoms had taken place in this instance. . . .

Within a few short years, elements of the law that had been touted as safeguards during the campaign to legalize assisted suicide were being depicted as barriers to be overcome.

Another reason for skepticism about Oregon's official claims that complications are limited to vomiting is the experience in the Netherlands where assisted-suicide complications and problems are not uncommon. For example, in 2000, two articles in the *New England Journal of Medicine (NEJM)* focused on those complications. One described a Dutch study that found that, because of problems or complications, doctors in the Netherlands felt compelled to intervene (by giving a lethal injection) in 18 percent of cases. This led Dr. Sherwin Nuland of Yale University to question the credibility of Oregon's lack of reported complications. Nuland, who favors physician-assisted suicide, noted that the Dutch have had years of practice to learn ways to overcome complications, yet complications are still reported. "The Dutch findings seem more credible [than the Oregon reports]," he wrote.

Deaths of Patients with Dementia

Official reports do not contain a category for assisted-suicide deaths of patients with dementia. Since Oregon law states that only "capable adults" (those who are able to make and communicate their health care decisions) are qualified to receive assisted suicide, it would seem that patients with dementia would not be "qualified patients." However, there is at least one account of a person with dementia dying after receiving a lethal overdose prescribed under the law: Kate Cheney, 85, died of assisted suicide under Oregon's law even though she reportedly was suffering from early dementia. Her own physician declined to provide the lethal prescription. When counseling to assess her capacity was sought, a psychiatrist determined that she was not eligible for assisted suicide since she was not explicitly seeking it, and her daughter seemed to be coaching her to do so. Also, she was unable to remember the name of her doctor or details of a hospital stay that month. She was then taken to a psychologist who found that she was competent but possibly under the influence of her daughter who was "somewhat coercive." Finally a managed care ethicist who was overseeing her case determined that she was qualified for assisted suicide, and the drugs were prescribed.

The tragic case of Ms. Cheney would never have come to light if her daughter had not contacted the *Oregonian* to express her outrage that legal safeguards had been roadblocks to her mother's death. Within a few short years, elements of the law that had been touted as safeguards during the campaign to legalize assisted suicide were being depicted as barriers to be overcome.

171

Deaths of Depressed Patients

Official Oregon reports contain no data regarding the number of depressed patients who have died of physician-assisted suicide. Yet, as with the case of patients with dementia, news accounts detail such deaths. . . .

Oregon's Medicaid program pays for assisted suicide but not for many other medical interventions that patients need and want.

The seventh annual report indicated that only 5 percent of patients were referred for a psychological evaluation or counseling before receiving a prescription for assisted suicide. Under the assisted-suicide law, depressed or mentally ill patients can receive assisted suicide if they do not have "impaired judgment." Concerning the decision to refer for a psychological evaluation, Oregon epidemiologist Dr. Mel Kohn told *American Medical News*, "According to the law, it's up to the docs' discretion."

Requests Based on Financial Concerns

Official reports state that six patients who died from assisted suicide since the law went into effect may have had financial concerns. However, data about reasons for requests is based on prescribing doctors' understanding of patients' motivations. It is possible that financial concerns were much greater than reported. According to official reports, 36 percent of patients whose deaths were reported were on Medicare (for senior citizens) or Medicaid (for the poor). However, after the second annual report, the reports have not differentiated between Medicare and Medicaid patients dying from assisted suicide. Oregon's Medicaid program pays for assisted suicide but not for many other medical interventions that patients need and want.

Prescribed More than Six Months Before

Official reports deleted this specific category after the second year report. Lethal prescriptions under the Oregon law are supposed to be limited to patients who have a life expectancy of six months or less. During the first two years, reports indicated that two people who had received the deadly overdose were still alive more than six months later. One patient was still alive 17 months after the lethal drugs were prescribed.

The DHS is not authorized to investigate how physicians determine their patients' diagnoses or life expectancies. If physicians are prescribing for patients who do not have a terminal condition, there is no way to find out since the same doctors who are violating the guidelines would have to report their own violations. As the second annual official report stated, "[N]oncompliance is difficult to assess because of the possible repercussions for noncompliant physicians reporting data to the division."

Doctor-Patient Relationship

Although Oregon's assisted-suicide law requires that at least two weeks elapse between the patient's first and last requests for lethal drugs, the physician who actually prescribes the drugs for assisted suicide need not be the same physician to whom the first request was made.

In the third through the seventh years, the doctor-patient relationship in some reported assisted-suicide cases was under one week. Thus, either some physicians are not complying with the two-week requirement or they stepped in to write an assisted-suicide prescription after other physicians refused.

After the third year, official reports stopped including the "First Physician Asked Agreed to Write Prescription" category. During the first three years that Oregon's assisted-suicide law was in effect, official reports indicated that 41 percent of doctors to whom the first request was made refused to write a prescription for the lethal overdose. Reasons for the refusal—

which could have included an assessment that the patient was not qualified or was not terminally ill—were not provided. . . .

When discussing official Oregon reports, any data should always be preceded with that all-important qualifying adjective, "reported."

As demonstrated above, Oregon's reports leave more questions than answers. One thing, however, is certain. Official reports contain only reported information. Therefore, it is inaccurate to state, "There have been 208 assisted-suicide deaths since Oregon's law went into effect" or "There have been six assisted-suicide requests based on financial concerns." It is accurate to state, "There have been 208 *reported* assisted-suicide deaths since Oregon's law went into effect" or "There have been six *reported* assisted-suicide requests based on financial concerns." When discussing official Oregon reports, any data should always be preceded with that all-important qualifying adjective, "reported." . . .

HMOs' Efforts to Facilitate Assisted Suicide

The unwillingness of many of Oregon's physicians to write lethal prescriptions led one HMO [health maintenance organization] to issue a plea for physicians to facilitate assisted suicide and has also resulted in an assisted-suicide advocacy organization's involvement in most assisted-suicide cases.

American Medical News reported on such an effort, describing how, on August 6, 2002, Administrator Robert Richardson, MD, of Oregon's Kaiser Permanente sent an e-mail to doctors affiliated with Kaiser, asking doctors to contact him if they were willing to act as the "attending physician" for patients requesting assisted suicide. According to the message, the HMO needed more willing physicians because "recently our ethics service had a situation where no attending MD could be found to assist an eligible member in implementing the law for three weeks. . . ."

Gregory Hamilton, MD, a Portland psychiatrist pointed out that the Kaiser message caused concern for several reasons. "This is what we've been worried about: Assisted suicide would be administered through HMOs and by organizations with a financial stake in providing the cheapest care possible," he said. Furthermore, despite promoters' claims that assisted suicide would be strictly between patients and their long-time, trusted doctors, the overt recruitment of physicians to prescribe the lethal drugs indicated that those claims were not accurate. Instead, "if someone wants assisted suicide, they go to an assisted-suicide doctor—not their regular doctor."

Kaiser's Northwest Regional Medical Director Allan Weiland, MD, called Hamilton's comments "ludicrous and insulting." However, it appears that Hamilton was correct, as the involvement of an assisted-suicide advocacy group indicates. . . .

Lack of Family Involvement

The lack of family involvement presents yet another red flag for anyone who might be inclined to favor an Oregon-type law. Under Oregon's law, family members do not need to be informed before a doctor helps a loved one commit suicide. Family notification is only recommended, but not required, under Oregon's assisted-suicide law. The first time that a family learns that a loved one was considering suicide could be after the death has occurred. . . .

Protection for Doctors

Under Oregon's law and in proposals made in other states, there are greater protections for doctors than for patients. While assisted-suicide advocates claim that patients are given new rights under Oregon's law, nothing could be farther from the truth. Prior to the law's passage, patients could request, but doctors could not provide, assisted suicide. It was illegal and unethical for a physician to knowingly participate in a patient's suicide. The law actually empowers doctors by promising them legal immunity if they provide a patient with an intentionally fatal prescription. Yet, advocates still say that the law grants patients a new legal right—the right to ask their doctors for suicide assistance, even though such a request was never illegal. Suicide requests from patients may have been cries for better pain control, support, or psychiatric help—but they were never crimes.

While assisted suicide may be a choice for the comfortably well off, it could become the only "medical treatment" that the poor can afford.

In addition, doctors who prescribe assisted suicide under Oregon's law are exempt from the standard of care that they are required to meet when providing other medical services. Under the assisted-suicide law, a health care provider is not subject to criminal or civil liability or any other professional disciplinary action as long as the provider is acting in "good faith." This subjective "good faith" standard is far less stringent than the objective "reasonable standard of care" that physicians are required to meet for compassionate medical care such as hospice, palliation, or curative treatment.

As a result, a doctor who negligently participates in assisted suicide cannot be held accountable so long as he or she claims to have acted in "good faith." On the other hand, a doctor who negligently provides other medical interventions can be held legally accountable in civil court regardless of his or her "good faith." Lowering the standard of care for assisted suicide could serve as an inducement for doctors to recommend assisted suicide over palliative care at the end of life.

Suicide Rate in Oregon Climbs

In a touch of tragic irony, Oregon recently became the first state to institute an elderly suicide prevention program. For years, suicide rates in western states have exceeded the national average, but the rate among older Oregonians is particularly high. According to Lisa Millet of the Oregon Department of Human Services—the same governmental body responsible for issuing official reports on Oregon's assisted-suicide law—about as many elderly Oregonians die each year from suicide as from car accidents. (It should be noted that deaths under Oregon's assisted-suicide law are not included in suicide statistics since the cause of death is officially considered to be the person's underlying condition.) State officials do not see any conflict between suicide prevention and support of assisted suicide, saying that the aim of the suicide prevention program is to prevent suicides among those who "still have years left to enjoy life."

Choice or Requirement?

Oregon's law and Oregon-style proposals in other states contain a requirement that, prior to writing a prescription for lethal drugs, a physician must inform the patient of alternatives such as comfort care, hospice care, and pain control. However, informing someone of an option does not mean that the patient will have the financial ability to obtain that alternative.

Devastating financial pressures could take place in a state like California if it were to legalize physician-assisted suicide. Bear in mind that there were six reported assisted-suicide deaths in Oregon because of financial concerns. Then consider the fact that the number of Californians who went without health insurance in 2002 was almost double Oregon's *entire state population.*

As was so tragically apparent during hurricane Katrina [which severely damaged the Gulf Coast in 2005], not everyone who was "informed" of evacuation routes had the resources to use those routes. Likewise, patients without health insurance or with inadequate health insurance may not be able to pay for the pain control that would help them. While assisted suicide may be a choice for the comfortably well off, it could become the only "medical treatment" that the poor can afford.

Doctors Are Negatively Affected by Assisting in Suicide

Kenneth R. Stevens Jr.

Kenneth R. Stevens Jr., is an emeritus professor at Oregon Health and Science University and vice president of Physicians for Compassionate Care.

When new treatments or procedures in medicine are developed, they are scrutinized to determine if there are adverse or harmful effects associated with them. In the same way, physician-assisted suicide [PAS] and euthanasia deserve to be evaluated to determine if they have adverse or harmful effects. Instead of focusing on the involved patients, this investigation focuses on the reported effects on the doctors who are involved in assisted suicide and euthanasia.

This investigation's focus is to determine what has been reported regarding the following questions:

- What have been the emotional and psychological effects of participation in PAS and euthanasia on the involved doctors?

- What have they expressed to others regarding their experiences?

- Are physicians being pressured, intimidated or psychologically influenced to assist in suicide or perform euthanasia?

Kenneth R. Stevens, "Emotional and Psychological Effects of Physician-Assisted Suicide and Euthanasia on Participating Physicians," *Issues in Law and Medicine*, Spring 2006, pp. 187–200. Reproduced by permission.

- What has happened to doctors who have written prescriptions? Have they continued to be involved with assisted suicide with other patients after the experience with the first patient or have they stopped their involvement?

Since the passage of Oregon's assisted suicide law in 1994, the author has gathered and archived articles from medical journals, legislative investigations, and the public press regarding assisted suicide and euthanasia. . . . These publications were reviewed and analyzed to obtain information regarding the above questions.

The Netherlands

Doctors in the Netherlands who have had experience with assisted suicide and euthanasia, have expressed concerns regarding the effects on doctors. A report from the Netherlands stated: "Many physicians who had practiced euthanasia mentioned that they would be most reluctant to do so again."

[Researcher E.J.] Emanuel stated that "in a television program reporting a euthanasia case, the Dutch physician who performed euthanasia noted that: 'To kill someone is something far reaching and that is something that nags at your conscience. . . . I wonder what it would be like not to have these cases in my practice. Perhaps I would be a much more cheerful person.'"

[Sixteen percent] of the physicians reported that the emotional burden of performing euthanasia or PAS adversely affected their medical practice.

The *American Medical News* reported the following comments from Pieter Admiraal, a leader of Holland's euthanasia movement: "'You will never get accustomed to killing somebody. We are not trained to kill. With euthanasia, your nightmare comes true.'"

In 1995–96, 405 Dutch doctors were interviewed regarding their feelings after their most recent case of euthanasia, assisted suicide, life ending without an explicit request, and alleviation of pain and other symptoms with high doses of opioids [narcotic drugs]. The percentage of doctors expressing feelings of discomfort were: 75% following euthanasia, 58% following assisted suicide, 34% following life ending without an explicit request, and 18% for alleviation of pain with high doses of opioids. Fifty percent of the euthanasias and 40% of the assisted suicides were followed by "burdensome" feelings; and 48% of the euthanasia and 49% of the assisted suicide cases were followed by emotional discomfort. The willingness to perform physician-assisted death again was 95% after euthanasia and 82% for life ending without an explicit request. The doctors sought support afterwards following 43% of the euthanasia cases and following 16% of cases involving ending life without an explicit request. . . .

The United States

Two surveys of physicians in the United States have examined and reported on the effects on physicians of performing PAS or euthanasia.

In a structured in-depth telephone interview survey of randomly selected United States oncologists who reported participating in euthanasia or PAS, Emanuel reported 53% of physicians received comfort from having helped a patient with euthanasia or PAS, 24% regretted performing euthanasia or PAS, and 16% of the physicians reported that the emotional burden of performing euthanasia or PAS adversely affected their medical practice.

In a mail survey of physicians who had acknowledged performing PAS or euthanasia, [researcher D.E.] Meier reported the following responses pertaining to the most recent patient who had received a prescription for a lethal dose of medication or a lethal injection among the 81 physician respondents

(47% were prescriptions, 53% were injections): 18% of the physicians reported being somewhat uncomfortable with their role in writing a prescription, and 6% were somewhat uncomfortable with the lethal injection; <1% were very uncomfortable with their role in writing the lethal prescription, and 6% were very uncomfortable with the lethal injection.

The State of Oregon

The first cases of legal PAS in Oregon occurred in 1998. In 2000, thirty-five Oregon physicians who had received requests for assisted suicide from patients were interviewed regarding their responses to such requests. Mixed feelings were expressed by the physicians. The authors noted: "Participation in assisted suicide required a large investment of time and had a strong emotional impact. . . . Even when they felt they had made appropriate choices, many physicians expressed uncertainty about how they would respond to requests in the future." . . .

A Dutch family physician and medical ethicist writes . . . that some professionals become dysfunctional and may require a lot of time to recover.

In 1998, the first year of Oregon's Death with Dignity Act, fourteen physicians wrote prescriptions for lethal medications for the fifteen patients who died from physician-assisted suicide. The annual report observed that: "For some of these physicians, the process of participating in physician-assisted suicide exacted a large emotional toll, as reflected by such comments as, 'It was an excruciating thing to do . . . it made me rethink life's priorities,' 'This was really hard on me, especially being there when he took the pills,' and 'This had a tremendous emotional impact.' Physicians also reported that their participation led to feelings of isolation. Several physicians expressed frustration that they were unable to share their experiences with others because they feared ostracism by patients and colleagues if they were known to have participated in physician-assisted suicide." This type of information regarding the emotional impact on the involved physicians has not been presented in subsequent Oregon annual reports.

A 1999 mail-survey of physicians' experiences with the Oregon Death with Dignity Act reported: "Some physicians who provided assistance with suicide under the Oregon Death with Dignity Act reported problems, including unwanted publicity, difficulty obtaining the lethal medication or a second opinion, difficulty understanding the requirements of the law, difficulties with hospice providers, not knowing the patient, or the absence of someone to discuss the situation with." "Four physicians expressed ambivalence about having provided assistance with the suicide, though two of the four noted that they had become less ambivalent over time. One of these physicians decided not to provide such assistance again." . . .

A Doctor's Account

Dr. Peter Reagan's description of his experience with "Helen" was the first individual account in the medical literature of assisted suicide in Oregon. His account reveals his emotional and psychological concerns. As Helen was dying from his prescribed lethal medication "[t]he three of us [Dr. Reagan and Helen's son and daughter] sat around her bed talking quietly about the emotional struggle we'd each been through." Regarding his thoughts and emotions leading up to writing the lethal prescription, Dr. Reagan wrote:

> I had to accept that this really was going to happen. Of course I could choose not to participate. The thought of Helen dying so soon was almost too much to bear, and only slightly less difficult was the knowledge that many very reasonable people would consider aiding in her death a crime. On the other hand, I found even worse the thought of disappointing this family. If I backed out, they'd feel about me the way they had about their previous doctor, that I had strung them along, and in a way, insulted them.

This is an example of a doctor feeling intimidated and coerced by the family and patient to participate in assisted suicide.

In writing about Helen's expressed appreciation for his role in the assisted suicide, Dr. Reagan wrote, "I thanked her and then turned away with my tangle of emotions." "That afternoon . . . I wrote the prescription for the 90 secobarbital. I hesitated at the signature and stared out the window. . . . I tried to imagine deciding to die. . . . Whenever I tried, I experienced a sadness much more profound than what I saw in her." "I slept badly."

The extent of Dr. Reagan's personal concerns is exemplified by his editorial inclusion of the following: "Experience in the Netherlands suggests that doctors are profoundly affected by an act of physician-assisted suicide. Gerrit Kimsma, a Dutch family physician and medical ethicist, writes with colleagues that some professionals become dysfunctional and may require a lot of time to recover." . . .

In a newspaper interview in 2001, [a] reporter wrote, "Dr. Peter Reagan, the primary physician in the first publicly described case in 1998, said the experience changed his feelings about assisted suicide. If he were dying, 'I made a commitment that I wouldn't ask my own doctor to help in this way,' Reagan said, 'because it's a lot to ask.'" Dr. Reagan described his troubled feelings in the reversal of his role as a healer, to his role in assisting Helen in her suicide. There is a sense of isolation. In Dr. Reagan's first comments to the public and press, he was concealed by anonymity. It was difficult for him to find others with whom to discuss his troubling experience.

[Medical ethicist Dr.] Leon Kass stated that "the psychological burden of the license to kill (not to speak of the brutalization of the physician-killers) could very well be an intolerably high price to pay for physician-assisted euthanasia."

The author of an investigation of "the euthanasia underground" reported:

The personal cost of involvement in illegal euthanasia was a central theme in interviews, and one emphasized throughout this book. 'I hate it', says one doctor, 'my partner hates it, because [she] feels that I'm going to be really horrible to be around ... afterwards.' Another emphasized the 'emotionally demanding and draining' nature of involvement, adding 'there's only a finite amount of times you can do it' and 'I think I've almost reached the expiry date.' These are typical comments.

[N.G.] Hamilton and [C.A.] Hamilton reviewed the first case of legal assisted suicide in Oregon that was reported in the press. The physician who helped the ill woman end her life described the woman's tenacity and determination in her decision. "It was like talking to a locomotive. It was like talking to Superman when he's going after a train." The Hamiltons' psychiatric analysis of this case was that the doctor felt helpless when faced with the challenge of containing a patient who elicited images of locomotives, or of attempting to make a therapeutic intervention when talking with the patient seemed, as he put it, like "talking to Superman when he's going after a train." The doctor was expressing powerlessness on his part.

This intimidation of doctors by patients who request assisted suicide is also described in an analysis of in-depth personal interviews of thirty-five Oregon physicians who received a request for a lethal prescription. The article portrays a daunting situation for the doctors. These doctors describe very forceful patients who persevered in their requests for assisted suicide, even when the doctors were unwilling to participate. One doctor quoted a patient as saying, "I am going to come in and I am going to try to convince you." Another doctor said, "I learned very quickly that the patient's agenda is to get the medication. When I tried to talk them out of it, or to really assess their motivations, then they perceived me as obstructionist and became quite resentful of that." ...

Lack of Data

After seven years [as of 2004] of legalized assisted suicide in Oregon, we should have answers to the following questions:

- What is the total number of physicians who have written prescriptions under Oregon's PAS law?

- What has been the pattern of prescribing? How many physicians have written only one prescription, and how many have written multiple prescriptions?

- Most importantly, are there physicians who have written prescriptions in earlier years, who are not now writing prescriptions? Why have they changed their minds, and are not now involved in assisted suicide?

The basic Oregon PAS data for the early years has been destroyed, as noted in the following personal communication: "Unfortunately, we are unable to provide any additional information than is currently available in our Annual Reports. Prior to 2001, we did collect the names of physicians who were participating. However, because of concerns about maintaining the confidentiality of participating physicians, we began using a numeric coding system in 2001. When we implemented this coding system, we destroyed the identifying data from the earlier years." . . .

Physician participation in assisted suicide or euthanasia may have a profound harmful emotional toll on the involved physicians.

Because this basic Oregon data was destroyed by personnel in the state agency, the answers to the above questions will never be known. . . .

During the first four years of legalized PAS in Oregon the prescribing physician was present at the time the patient took the lethal medication for 52% of the assisted suicides. However during the 2004 year, the prescribing physician was present for only 16% of the patients. Why are the physicians withdrawing from being present at the time of the assisted suicide?

Countertransference

Countertransference is defined as a phenomenon referring "to the attitudes and feelings, only partly conscious, of the analyst towards the patient." Regarding the "rational" decision of physicians to assist in the ending of a person with a terminal illness, Dr. Glen O. Gabbard, a noted psychiatrist, has written:

> Those decisions made by medical professionals, including psychiatrists, can never be entirely free of what we would broadly call countertransference issues. The doctor's own anxiety in the face of death, and even the hatred of the patient who does not want treatment or will not allow the doctor to be helpful, can influence a supposedly scientific or "rational" decision.

The involvement of countertransference with assisted suicide has been evaluated by [F.T.] Varghese and [R.] Kelly. They report that:

> [T]he subjective evaluation by a doctor of a patient's 'quality of life' and the role of such an evaluation in making end-of-life decisions of themselves raise significant countertransference issues. Inaccurately putting oneself 'in the patient's shoes' in order to make clinical decisions and evaluations of quality of life leave the patient vulnerable to the doctor's personal and unrecognized issues concerning illness, death and disability.

They state that "[f]ortunately, the ethical code prohibits certain actions on the part of the doctor. In the absence of these prohibitions, the doctor's countertransference feelings about patients could put the public in grave danger." They conclude "Psychopathological factors in the doctor, including reactions to illness, death, and the failure of treatment, can influence the dying patient's end-of-life decision."

Physician participation in assisted suicide or euthanasia may have a profound harmful emotional toll on the involved physicians. Doctors must take responsibility for causing the patient's death. There is a huge burden on conscience, tangled emotions and a large psychological toll on the participating physicians. Many physicians describe feelings of isolation. Published evidence indicates that some patients and others are pressuring and intimidating doctors to assist in suicides. Some doctors feel they have no choice but to be involved in assisted suicides. Oregon physicians are decreasingly present at the time of the assisted suicide. There is also great potential for physicians to be affected by countertransference issues in dealing with end-of-life care, and assisted suicide and euthanasia.

These significant adverse "side effects" on the doctors participating in assisted suicide and euthanasia need to be considered when discussing the pros and cons of legalization.

Volunteers Are Assisting in Suicides Where It Is Not Legal

Paul Rubin

Paul Rubin is a reporter for the Phoenix New Times.

Last spring [2007], family and friends gathered at a service for Jana Van Voorhis, a 58-year-old Phoenix woman who recently had died at her home. . . .

At the conclusion, Jana's family released helium-filled blue balloons into the air, something she had requested years earlier during what often had been a tortured existence marred by chronic mental illness.

Never married, Jana was well-loved by her family, including her two siblings, Viki Thomas of Phoenix and Wes Van Voorhis, a Seattle-area physician and University of Washington professor.

On the afternoon of April 15, Viki and her husband, Jared, found Jana's body in bed. . . . They immediately suspected her death had been caused by a drug overdose, intentional or not. Those close to Jana knew she had a veritable apothecary of prescribed painkillers, sleep inducers, and mood stabilizers on hand.

But the couple noted that there wasn't a pill bottle in sight, which seemed odd to them. Also, Jana's body had been neatly tucked under the covers, her hands by her side atop the sheets, dark hair carefully fanned out on a pillow. "It looked staged," Viki Thomas says.

A few months later, after the circumstances of what actually had been Jana Van Voorhis' *assisted* suicide emerged, the image of the balloons at the service struck Jared Thomas (whom everyone calls Tom). "When those balloons were float-

Paul Rubin, "Death Wish," *Phoenix New Times*, August 23, 2007. Reproduced by permission of Village Voice Media.

ing off, we didn't have a clue that helium had killed Jana," he says. "To think of her breathing in helium from a tank while two strangers just stood by and watched; it's just too much."

Manslaughter Charges May Be Filed

Maricopa County [Arizona] prosecutors are contemplating whether to file manslaughter charges against two senior citizens who have admitted to guiding Jana Van Voorhis through her suicide on April 12.

Arizona law makes it a crime to intentionally aid another person in committing suicide. But the prosecution would be a first in the state of Arizona, in part because the word "aid" is fraught with legal uncertainties in such circumstances. Convictions would be anything but a slam dunk, but the facts in this case are extremely disturbing. . . .

Primary sources for this story include extensive police reports about the case, and *New Times'* interviews with Jana's family and with one of the two so-called exit guides from a national assisted-suicide group who were present when Jana died.

Final Exit Network is considered among the most radical of the assisted-suicide associations, in that it also embraces "members" who suffer from serious mental illnesses, not just physical.

That "senior" guide was Wye Hale-Rowe, 79, a retired family therapist and great-grandmother from Aurora, Colorado. The title refers to her experience in the field, not her age. The second guide was Frank Langsner, a retired college professor who lives in Scottsdale.

They are volunteers for the nonprofit Final Exit Network, an offshoot of the now-defunct Hemlock Society, which was founded in 1980 by author Derek Humphrey. The Hemlock Society moved into the American consciousness in the late

1980s, some years before Dr. Jack Kevorkian's high-profile run of assisting in more than 100 suicides became headline news.

Humphrey's bestselling book, *Final Exit: The Practicalities of Self-Deliverance and Assisted Suicide for the Dying*, was published in 1991 and still sells well. One of its pitches: "Follow my instructions for a perfect death, with no mess, no autopsy, no postmortem."

Based in Marietta, Georgia, Final Exit Network is considered among the most radical of the assisted-suicide associations, in that it also embraces "members" who suffer from serious mental illnesses, not just physical [ones]. . . .

In its literature, Final Exit calls itself "the only organization in the United States willing to help individuals who are *not* 'terminally ill'—six months or less to live—hasten their deaths. No other organization in the U.S. has the courage to make this commitment."

That bold statement is what may have attracted Jana Van Voorhis.

Records suggest she first contacted Final Exit last year [2006], paid the $50 to join, and sought its help in dying sooner than later. Helping meant teaching Jana the creepy how-to of inhaling helium after placing a hood tightly over her face.

Jana's Illness Was Mental

Though she did have physical issues, Jana (according to family members and medical records) wasn't suffering from any illness about to kill her anytime soon. What Jana was suffering from, and had been for decades, was serious mental illness.

Since her teenage years, Jana's problems had required intensive psychiatric care. Her troubles increased over time, especially after her mother became incapacitated with Alzheimer's disease and died in July 2006. By mid-2006, according to notes made by Jana's final psychiatrist, Dr. Michael Fermo, she "had been increasingly becoming psychotic, claiming the roof rats have been overtaking her home, sneaking into her house, and attacking her."

Even if it seems obvious to shrinks and the public that someone is "crazy," he or she still may not qualify legally as incompetent.

According to Final Exit Network's written criteria, each applicant "must be mentally competent" before exit guides get the go-ahead to assist with a suicide (they call it aid-in-dying, hastening death, or another term that doesn't invoke the inflammatory "S" word).

Some experts contend that *anyone* desiring to commit suicide, especially a person not suffering from a fatal illness, may be considered mentally incompetent.

Precisely defining incompetence, however, is dicey. For starters, mental health diagnoses and legal definitions often do not jibe. Even if it seems obvious to shrinks and the public that someone is "crazy," he or she still may not qualify legally as incompetent.

Final Exit Network's protocol also demands that someone who desires to commit suicide "must attest that all relevant family members or caregivers will not interfere with your wishes." The network also claims it will not assist in a suicide "when family, friends or caregivers know about the patient's plans and are strongly opposed."

The network doesn't address what happens when a member is estranged from his or her family and doesn't want it involved in the so-called death event. In this instance, no one from the network ever contacted Jana's family to get their position on her apparent death wish. Instead, her exit guides abided by Jana's alleged wishes and kept the suicide plan hush-hush to the end. Jana's closest family members insist they would have done anything to stop her from killing herself— had they known what was up.

Wye Hale-Rowe, who long has been prominent in the assisted-suicide movement, tells *New Times* she doesn't believe that Jana was seriously mentally ill. "Jana was in the throes of what we call existential suffering," says Hale-Rowe. "Even though their physical pain may be managed, just being alive is a burden. They're not able to function much with reference to other people.

"Jana knew what it was like to have had a very functional, active life, and that was part of her angst, that she had lost it and there was no way she could get any of it back." . . .

Volunteers Helped Her Plan Suicide

Neither of the exit guides knew Jana Van Voorhis before she contacted the organization and pleaded for its assistance in doing herself in. The sum of Wye Hale-Rowe's "relationship" with Jana was a suicide practice session on the day Jana died and then a few minutes of dialogue before Jana killed herself.

Hale-Rowe's colleague, Frank Langsner, did spend time with Jana in the weeks before the April [2007] "death event" (as Final Exit Network calls it), starting at a February "intake interview."

"You never, ever encourage someone to hasten their own deaths. It's entirely their choice."

In a June 6 taped interview with a Phoenix homicide detective, Langsner focused on Jana's physical ailments rather than her deep-seated mental issues. He claimed she'd been long-suffering from lung and back pain, possible breast cancer, an alleged lesion on her liver, and other problems. Langsner apparently took Jana at her word because her medical records don't reveal a terminal illness or anything that serious physically.

"She had no relationship with her family," Langsner told the detectives. "She had nothing to do with her sister and she had a brother in Seattle. She was all alone. She didn't even bother with her neighbors. . . . This was a person who wanted to die."

To help Jana succeed, Frank Langsner said, "You help get them in a frame of mind that they want to do it."

If the lead detective on the case got that quote right, it may well prove legally damning to Langsner. (The quote comes directly from a police report. *New Times* did not hear the actual interview, and the cops won't discuss the ongoing investigation.)

In stark contrast to Langsner, Wye Hale-Rowe says, "You never, ever encourage someone to hasten their own deaths. It's entirely their choice. You're only there because they've expressed this wish. Many people back off at the last minute, which is absolutely no problem for me." . . .

Langsner's allegation that Jana's family had "no relationship" with her is ludicrous to Viki Thomas. Viki, who lives about three miles from Jana's townhouse, says she spoke with her sister almost daily, including on the day of the suicide.

Viki's increasingly worried calls to Jana before she and her husband found Jana's decaying body were preserved on an answering-machine message now in police custody.

"My sister had problems from early on, but her family loved her, and she knew it," Viki Thomas says. "For anyone to say otherwise is just wrong, I can't imagine how Jana felt in her head. But we think that if these people [Final Exit Network] hadn't come into her life, she wouldn't have done what she did."

That said, if Jana *had* lived, her increasingly severe delusions and paranoia might have led to an involuntary commitment in a psychiatric hospital, a lousy fate.

But did that give the Final Exit guides any right to become her Johnny-on-the-spot suicide advisors?

Wye Hale-Rowe wavers when asked to compare someone's overwhelming *physical* suffering to unbearable *mental* suffering. "I'm not one to say we should treat mental illness the same as physical, because it's too easy to say and too hard to do," she says. "We're on pretty shaky ground, I think, and we have to be very, very careful in this area. I just went into a risky case, and now I'm stuck with what happened."

But equating Jana's mental despair with that of a person suffering a terminal physical disease is what Final Exit Network did. That and the failure of the exit guides to speak with Jana's family are what is at issue here. . . .

During searches of the homes of the two exit guides present during Jana's suicide, detectives found copies of the "intake interview" with Jana, dated February 17, [2007,] and a Final Exit form letter, which Jana initialed on March 24 and then again on the day she died. That letter includes this statement: "Physicians have determined that I have a terminal or hopeless illness, with no expectation of improvement. . . . My present condition is intolerable. I therefore seek information to help me explore my options for a hastened death."

Serious mental illness may last a lifetime, and, in that way, could be termed a "hopeless" condition.

But being profoundly depressed seems different from hopelessness endured by someone that, say, can't move a muscle because of a neurodegenerative disease.

Jana also inscribed her initials next to the following sentence in Final Exit's form letter: "I have considered the feelings of my family, friends and other loved ones, and have decided to choose the time and manner of my death. No one has tried to make this choice. It is entirely my own." . . .

When Langsner finally admitted his key role in Jana's suicide to Phoenix police, he said he'd reminded Jana about another network "rule." That, according to Final Exit's Web site, is "You must be able to procure the items required for your use [in a suicide]."

Jana had enough pills at her townhouse to bring down a small team of horses, so she really didn't have to procure anything. But Final Exit Network prefers self-asphyxiation by inhaling helium through a hose, with an oxygen-eliminating hood snugly over one's head. . . .

Jack Kevorkian's second-degree murder conviction in 1999 aside, prosecutions of those who assist in suicides are rare nationwide.

Langsner advised Jana to contact a local party-supply store and order helium tanks, which normally are used for filling balloons. He also recommended that Jana order by mail the special hood said to be ideal for the bleak task of committing suicide by helium.

Final Exit literature says its exit guides are prosecution-proof if they follow this one-step-removed approach to assisting in suicides of its members. Maricopa County prosecutors may have something to say about that. . . .

An Experienced Guide

Though she'd said little to the Phoenix cops, Hale-Rowe recently spoke to *New Times* twice for this story. In those interviews, she came across as thoughtful and quick-witted, but also deeply conflicted about what happened in Phoenix on April 12 [2007] and concerned about her own future.

She says her interest in assisted suicide had started long ago, when she was a girl growing up as a rancher's daughter. There, she says, sick animals were routinely euthanized to spare them needless physical suffering. But when Hale-Rowe's mother became terminally ill and begged for help, nothing legally could be done to "hasten" her death.

Hale-Rowe says she got involved with the Hemlock Society after it was founded by Derek Humphrey in 1980. She is considered one of the national right-to-die movement's most experienced advocates.

Still, she says, "This cause has been just a part of my life, certainly not my whole life. I've been ushered through a killer disease [she's a cancer survivor], and I've been kept alive and in reasonably good health to such an old age. I have a lot of things going on, and things I have been looking forward to.

"But not everyone has been so lucky as me. Maybe we have a more enlightened vision these days, because we don't blame people for wanting to die anymore. Some of them can be made much more comfortable and can enjoy living and stay around for a long time. But others really can't, and Jana was one of them. She wasn't getting better, and she could have been sent to some kind of facility and lived another 20 years—miserably." . . .

[Notorious assisted-suicide practitioner, Dr.] Jack Kevorkian's second-degree murder conviction in 1999 aside, prosecutions of those who assist in suicides are rare nation-wide—and are unprecedented in Arizona.

One issue bound to arise inside the County Attorney's Office as prosecutors decide whether to charge Langsner and Hale-Rowe is this: Anytime you are in the presence of someone breaking the law and you aid them in committing a crime, you may be held criminally liable as an accomplice. It's called "accomplice liability." Classic examples are being a lookout for a robber, providing guns or other instruments of crime, driving a getaway vehicle, and so on.

But it's not against the law to kill oneself. So, how can someone who goes along with another person's suicide be convicted of manslaughter by "aiding" an act that's not a crime? . . .

Viki and Tom Thomas say they'd never given much thought to the ins and outs of assisted suicide before Jana died. Now, the couple say they aren't against the concept under certain circumstances, such as when someone really is dying and is in great pain and wants to speed up the inevitable.

But Jana's case, they say, feels different to them, and not just because she was family and now she's gone.

"If the Final Exit Network had gotten ahold of me, I would have called Jana and gotten right over there," Viki Thomas says. "Sure, she had problems. But she was alive, and now she's not."

Assisted Suicides in Public Places Spur Protests in Switzerland

DPA News

DPA is an international news agency headquartered in Hamburg, Germany, that supplies news and information to organizations around the world.

The Swiss Dignitas organization has long been controversial for its assisted suicides and the legal grey area that practice inhabits. However, a report on Swiss television on the assisted suicide of two Germans at a car park in the woodlands near Zurich has caused a fresh storm of protest.

The two men, aged 50 and 65 years and from the southern German states of Bavaria and Baden-Wuerrtemberg across the Swiss border, took their lives in a car in a parking lot in the town of Maur, east of the city of Zurich.

Active euthanasia is banned in Switzerland. However, under Swiss law a terminally ill person wanting to die can be offered a poison, which they then take voluntarily.

The mayor of the 9,000-strong community of Maur, Bruno Sauter, has called the car deaths "impious and distasteful."

It is not the first time Sauter has encountered assisted suicide. Dignitas founder Ludwig Minelli, 75, lives in his district and Minelli is said to have earlier permitted a German woman to die in her car in front of his house, *Blick* newspaper reported on [November 7, 2007].

"Now Dignitas has gone too far," a Swiss legislator said on the radio, while also announcing new initiatives against "dying tourism." Minelli issued a statement rejecting the accusations.

DPA News, "Has Swiss Euthanasia Group Dignitas Gone Too Far?" EarthTimes.org, November 8, 2007. Copyright © 2007 DPA. Reproduced by permission.

Even undertaker Urs Gerber, who is otherwise prepared to admit that one has to "put up with a lot" in his line of business, criticizes the car park deaths. He speaks of "undignified surrounding conditions," for instance when he has to pull the bodies out of the car and stretch them out on the ground.

Many think it likely that Minelli wanted to cause provocation. After all, Dignitas has constantly been in the headlines over the past weeks because more and more communities in the Zurich area had been refusing to give their permission for the so-called dying rooms in rented apartments.

Critics want organizations like Dignitas to be licensed, and they demand "quality standards" and stricter supervision of their activities.

This is where the Dignitas boss used to take his clients to receive their deadly poisoned cocktail. The clients have to take the cocktail themselves, fully aware of what they are doing.

Neighborhoods Object

Many residential areas have seen protests because there was a constant stream of ambulances and hearses, so Dignitas finally moved into industrial estates. However, there were protests there too.

Then the organization began to use hotels, only to find their owners appeal to Minelli to leave them alone.

So now it's a car park in the woodlands.

Sauter wants to prevent another incident like this with the help of his watchful citizens. However, public prosecutor Juerg Vollenweider doesn't see a chance to stop such a public suicide. "Those who want to die outdoors or in their beloved car are free to do so," he says. The law is clear on that and Minelli knows that too.

However, there are also dissenting voices. Supporters of euthanasia say euthanasia organizations can help people to die in dignity who would otherwise not be able to do so.

"It is part of a self-determined life to have a self-determined death in dignity as well," Urs Lauffer, a legislator from Zurich, says.

The numerous local parliamentary initiatives to prevent the practice from getting out of hand could soon be followed by an initiative in the chambers of the national parliament.

Critics want organizations like Dignitas to be licensed, and they demand "quality standards" and stricter supervision of their activities.

Those who demand better controls are backed by reports that people willing to die were left to suffer for a long time because the natrium pentobarbital [drug] that was administered had not worked properly. Some 15 grams of the strong soporific are dissolved in water.

Minelli fundamentally rejected any such accusations in a letter to the *Neue Zuercher Zeitung* daily [newspaper] in one of his rare public statements.

However, he admitted that there were a few incidents—"maybe one in several hundred"—in which it took a long time for someone to die. But there was no apparent reason for it.

The paper wrote that experts found this hard to understand. Hans Muralt, branch manager of the euthanasia organization Exit in Zurich, told the paper that he was not aware of anyone having suffered during his long time in the office.

Organizations to Contact

The editors have compiled the following list of organizations concerned with the issues debated in this book. The descriptions are derived from materials provided by the organizations. All have publications or information available for interested readers. The list was compiled on the date of publication of the present volume; the information provided here may change. Be aware that many organizations take several weeks or longer to respond to inquiries, so allow as much time as possible.

Americans for Better Care of the Dying (ABCD)
1700 Diagonal Rd., Suite 635, Alexandria, VA   22314
(703) 647-8505 • fax: (703) 837-1233
e-mail: info@abcd-caring.org
Web site: www.abcd-caring.org

ABCD aims to improve end-of-life care by learning which social and political changes will lead to enduring, efficient, and effective programs. It focuses on improved pain management, better financial reimbursement systems, enhanced continuity of care, support for family caregivers, and changes in public policy. Its Web site offers current news, online action guides, and an electronic version of *Handbook for Mortals*, a consumer guide to end-of-life care.

Care Not Killing Alliance
PO Box 56322, London   SE1 8XW
  UK
e-mail: info@carenotkilling.org.uk
Web site: www.carenotkilling.org.uk

Care Not Killing is a United Kingdom–based alliance of individuals and organizations that brings together human rights groups, health-care groups, palliative-care groups, and faith-based organizations with the aims of promoting more and better palliative care and ensuring that existing laws against euthanasia and assisted suicide are not weakened or repealed. Its Web site contains articles opposing legalization, news, and information about legislation pending in the United Kingdom.

Caring Connections
National Hospice and Palliative Care Organization
Alexandria, Virginia   22314
(703) 837-1500 • fax: (703) 837-1233
e-mail: caringinfo@nhpco.org
Web site: www.nhpco.org

Caring Connections, a program of the National Hospice and Palliative Care Organization (NHPCO), is a national consumer engagement initiative to improve care at the end of life. Its Web site does not mention euthanasia or physician-assisted suicide; however, it contains detailed information about advance directives and about reasons why provision of artificial nutrition and hydration may increase a patient's suffering.

Citizens United Resisting Euthanasia (CURE)
303 Truman St., Berkeley Springs, WV   25411
(304) 258-5433
e-mail: cureltd@verizon.net
Web site: http://mysite.verizon.net/cureltd/index.html

CURE is a grassroots network of patient advocates from a broad range of professional, political, and religious backgrounds bound together in a common cause: uncompromising opposition to euthanasia and assisted suicide. It also opposes living wills (advance directives that authorize withholding of medical treatment), because it rejects the concept of brain death and organ donation. Its Web site contains a number of articles on these topics.

Compassion & Choices
PO Box 101810, Denver, CO   80250-1810
(800) 247-7421 • fax: 303-639-1224

e-mail: info@compassionandchoices.org
Web site: www.compassionandchoices.org

This is the oldest and largest choice-in-dying organization in the nation, created by the unification of Compassion in Dying and End-of-Life Choices, which was the successor to the Hemlock Society. It works for improved care and expanded options at the end of life, advocating comprehensive pain control and palliative care with legal aid in dying if suffering is unbearable. Volunteers in its many local groups provide free counseling and other services to individuals facing terminal illness and their families, as well as to those simply planning for the future. It publishes a monthly magazine and offers recommended publications for sale on its Web site.

Death with Dignity National Center
520 SW Sixth Ave., Suite 1030, Portland, OR   97204
(503) 228-4415 • fax: (503) 228-7454
e-mail: use online form
Web site: www.deathwithdignity.org

This nonpartisan, nonprofit organization has led the legal defense and education of the Oregon Death with Dignity Act and supports those seeking to pass similar laws in other states. Its Web site provides extensive information and links, with emphasis on the needs of student researchers and tips for getting the most from the resources provided.

Dying with Dignity
55 Eglinton Ave. East, Suite 802, Toronto, ON   M4P 1G8
  Canada
(800) 495-6156 • fax: (416) 486-5562
e-mail: info@dyingwithdignity.ca
Web site: www.dyingwithdignity.ca

The mission of this Canadian organization is to improve the quality of dying for all Canadians in accordance with their own wishes, values, and beliefs. It informs and educates individuals about their rights, provides counseling and advocacy services to members, and works to build public support for the legalization of voluntary physician-assisted dying. General information, with emphasis on Canadian issues, can be found on its Web site.

Euthanasia Research and Guidance Organization (ERGO)
24829 Norris La., Junction City, OR   97448
(541) 998-1873 • (541) 998-1873
e-mail: ergo@efn.org
Web sites: www.finalexit.org; www.assistedsuicide.org

ERGO is a nonprofit educational corporation established by Derek Humphry, founder of the former Hemlock Society. It is a strong advocate of assisted suicide and self-deliverance for people who are suffering from incurable illness. Its Web sites include essays and a blog by Humphry plus information about assisted-suicide laws around the world. Humphry's books are also offered for sale through the sites.

Exit International
PO Box 37781, Darwin, NT   0821
   Australia
e-mail: contact@exitinternational.net
Web site: www.exitinternational.net

Exit International was established by Philip Nitschke, an Australian doctor who is a strong proponent of legal euthanasia and assisted suicide and who was the first to perform euthanasia during a short period when it was legal in Australia. The organization believes that rational elderly people have the right to determine for themselves when and how they will die regardless of their state of health. Its volunteers provide counseling, but not assistance with suicide. An e-mail newsletter is sent to members and recent editions are available at its Web site, along with information about Dr. Nitschke and his views.

Final Exit Network
PO Box 965005, Marietta, GA   30066
(800) 524-3948

e-mail: info@finalexitnetwork.org
Web site: www.finalexitnetwork.org

Final Exit Network is an all-volunteer group dedicated to serving people who are suffering from an intolerable condition. These volunteers offer counseling, support, and even guidance in self-deliverance. It is the only organization in America that will help to hasten death for individuals not classed as terminally ill. Its Web site contains informational and detailed statistics from a recent poll concerning public attitudes toward end-of-life issues.

Growth House
2215-R Market St., Suite 199
San Francisco, California   94114
(415) 863-3045
e-mail: info@growthhouse.org
Web site: www.growthhouse.org

Growth House is a gateway to resources for life-threatening illness and end-of-life care. Its primary mission is to improve the quality of compassionate care for people who are dying through public education and global professional collaboration. It is neutral on the issue of euthanasia and assisted suicide. The Web site has extensive information on end-of-life subjects and links to other sites, including blogs, where these subjects are discussed. It also offers online discussion lists for health-care professionals.

Hastings Center
21 Malcolm Gordon Rd., Garrison, NY   10524-4125
(845) 424-4040 • fax: (845) 424-4545
e-mail: mail@thehastingscenter.org
Web site: www.thehastingscenter.org

The Hastings Center is an independent, nonpartisan, and nonprofit bioethics research institute that addresses fundamental and emerging questions in health care, biotechnology, and the environment, including those concerning euthanasia and assisted suicide. It publishes a bimonthly journal, the *Hastings Report*, and many other reports and essays, some of which can be viewed at its Web site.

Hospice Patients Alliance (HPA)

4541 Gemini St., Rockford, MI   49341-0744
(616) 866-9127
e-mail: patientadvocates@hospicepatients.org
Web site: www.hospicepatients.org

HPA provides information about hospice services; assists patients, families, and caregivers in resolving difficulties they may have with current hospice services; and promotes better quality hospice care throughout the United States. It is opposed to euthanasia and assisted suicide and believes that in many cases hospice patients are being subjected to what amounts to involuntary euthanasia. Its Web site contains many articles about this issue.

International Task Force on Euthanasia and Assisted Suicide

PO Box 760, Steubenville, OH   43952
(740) 282-3810
e-mail: use online form
Web site: http://iaetf.org

The International Task Force on Euthanasia and Assisted Suicide is a nonprofit educational and research organization that addresses end-of-life issues from a public policy perspective. It is opposed to euthanasia, assisted suicide, and living wills that give doctors the power to decide when to end treatment. Its Web site offers many articles about these issues, including a detailed frequently-asked-questions list presenting the case against assisted suicide.

Not Dead Yet

7521 Madison St., Forest Park, IL   60130
(708) 209-1500 • fax: (708) 209-1735
e-mail: ndycoleman@aol.com
Web site: www.notdeadyet.org

Not Dead Yet is a national grassroots disability rights organization. It was developed to oppose physician-assisted suicide, which if accepted as public policy would, in Not Yet Dead's view, single out individuals for legalized killing based on their health status and thus endanger disabled people. It also opposes withdrawal of life support from unconscious patients. Its Web site contains detailed material about related court cases as well as many other articles and a blog.

**Physicians for Compassionate Care
Educational Foundation (PCCEF)**
PO Box 6042, Portland, OR   97228-6042
(503) 533-8154 • fax: (503) 533-0429
e-mail: physiciansforcompassionatecare@verizon.net
Web site: www.pccef.org

Physicians for Compassionate Care is an association of physicians and other health professionals dedicated to preserving the traditional relation of the physician and patient as one in which the physician's primary task is to heal the patient and to minimize pain. It promotes compassionate care for severely ill patients without sanctioning or assisting their suicide. Its Web site contains many articles by members explaining their reasons for opposing Oregon's assisted suicide law and the passage of similar laws elsewhere.

Right to Die Society of Canada
145 Macdonell Ave., Toronto, ON   M6R 2A4
  Canada
(416) 535-0690 • fax: (416) 530-0243
e-mail: contact-rtd@righttodie.ca
Web site: www.righttodie.ca

This organization lobbies for the legalization of assisted suicide in Canada, educates the public, and presents a complete range of end-of-life options, including self-deliverance, to people who consult it. Its Web site offers articles and back issues of a newsletter.

Vermont Alliance for Ethical Healthcare
PO Box 2145, South Burlington, VT   05407-2145
(802) 658-0518
e-mail: info@vaeh.org
Web site: www.vaeh.org

The purpose of the Vermont Alliance for Ethical Healthcare is to promote the provision of excellent health care at the end of life in an ethical manner and to oppose efforts to legalize physician-assisted suicide or euthanasia in Vermont. Its Web site contains archives of past newsletters, information about physician-assisted suicide, including poll results, and lists of organizations that oppose the practice.

World Federation of Right to Die Societies
PO Box 570, Mill Valley, CA   94942
(415) 332-18104 • fax: (415) 332-18104
e-mail: worldfed@pacbell.net
Web site: www.worldrtd.net

This federation of thirty-seven member organizations from twenty-three countries believes that individuals should have the right to make their own choices as to the manner and timing of their own death. It responds to requests by groups, scholars, and individuals seeking information about various right-to-die issues. It publishes a newsletter, available on its Web site, several times a year. The site also contains links to articles, news reports, and other right-to-die sites.

Bibliography

Books

Robert M. Baird and Stuart E. Rosenbaum, eds. *Caring for the Dying: Critical Issues at the End of Life*. Amherst, NY: Prometheus, 2003.

Margaret Pabst Battin *Ending Life: Ethics and the Way We Die*. New York: Oxford University Press, 2005.

Nigel Biggar *Aiming to Kill: The Ethics of Suicide and Euthanasia*. Cleveland: Pilgrim, 2004.

Robert H. Blank and Janna C. Merrick, eds. *End-of-Life Decision Making: A Cross-National Study*. Cambridge, MA: MIT Press, 2005.

George M. Burnell *Freedom to Choose: How to Make End-of-Life Decisions on Your Own Terms*. Amityville, NY: Baywood, 2008.

Ian Dowbiggin *A Concise History of Euthanasia: Life, Death, God, and Medicine*. Lanham, MD: Rowman & Littlefield, 2005.

Ian Dowbiggin *A Merciful End: The Euthanasia Movement in Modern America*. New York: Oxford University Press, 2003.

Kathleen Foley and Herbert Hendin, eds. *The Case Against Assisted Suicide: For the Right to End-of-Life Care*. Baltimore: Johns Hopkins University Press, 2002.

Elizabeth Atwood Gailey — *Write to Death: News Framing the Right to Die Conflict from Quinlan's Coma to Kevorkian's Conviction.* Westport, CT: Praeger, 2003.

Neil M. Gorsuch — *The Future of Assisted Suicide and Euthanasia.* Princeton, NJ: Princeton University Press, 2006.

John Hardwig — *Is There a Duty to Die? and Other Essays in Bioethics.* New York: Routledge, 2000.

James M. Humber and Robert F. Almeder, eds. — *Is There a Duty to Die?* Totowa, NJ: Humana, 2000.

Derek Humphry — *The Good Euthanasia Guide 2004: Where, What, and Who in Choices in Dying.* Junction City, OR: Norris Lane, 2004.

Robert P. Jones — *Liberalism's Troubled Search for Equality: Religion and Cultural Bias in the Oregon Physician-Assisted Suicide Debates.* Notre Dame, IN: University of Notre Dame Press, 2007.

Albert R. Jonsen — Bioethics Beyond the Headlines: *Who Lives? Who Dies? Who Decides?* Lanham, MD: Rowman & Littlefield, 2005.

Shai J. Lavi — *The Modern Art of Dying: A History of Euthanasia in the United States.* Princeton, NJ: Princeton University Press, 2005.

Barbara Coombs Lee, ed.	*Compassion in Dying: Stories of Dignity and Choice.* Troutdale, OR: NewSage, 2003.
Penney Lewis	*Assisted Dying and Legal Change.* New York: Oxford University Press, 2007.
Roger S. Magnusson	*Angels of Death: Exploring the Euthanasia Underground.* New Haven, CT: Yale University Press, 2002.
John B. Mitchell	*Understanding Assisted Suicide: Nine Issues to Consider.* Ann Arbor: University of Michigan Press, 2007.
Philip Nitschke and Fiona Stewart	*Killing Me Softly: Voluntary Euthanasia and the Road to the Peaceful Pill.* New York: Penguin, 2005.
Suzanne Ost	*An Analytical Study of the Legal, Moral, and Ethical Aspects of the Living Phenomenon of Euthanasia.* Lewiston, NY: Edwin Mellen, 2003.
Craig Paterson	*Assisted Suicide and Euthanasia: A Natural Law Ethics Approach.* Burlington, VT: Ashgate, 2008.
Timothy E. Quill and Margaret P. Battin, eds.	*Physician-Assisted Dying: The Case for Palliative Care and Patient Choice.* Baltimore: Johns Hopkins University Press, 2004.
Phillip H. Robinson	*Euthanasia and Assisted Suicide.* South Bend, IN: Linacre Centre, 2004.

Barry Rosenfeld — *Assisted Suicide and the Right to Die: The Interface of Social Science, Public Policy, and Medical Ethics.* Washington, DC: American Psychological Association, 2004.

Wesley J. Smith — *Forced Exit: Euthanasia, Assisted Suicide and the New Duty to Die.* San Francisco: Encounter, 2006.

Stanley A. Terman — *The Best Way to Say Goodbye: A Legal Peaceful Choice at the End of Life.* Carlsbad, CA: Life Transitions, 2005.

Mary Warnock and Elisabeth Macdonald — *Easeful Death: Is There a Case for Assisted Suicide?* New York: Oxford University Press, 2008.

Periodicals

Jacob M. Appel — "A Suicide Right for the Mentally Ill? A Swiss Case Opens a New Debate," *Hastings Center Report*, May 1, 2007.

Julian Baggini and Madeleine Pym — "End-of-Life: The Humanist View," *Lancet*, October 1, 2005.

Daniel Bergner — "Death in the Family," *New York Times*, December 2, 2007.

Eric Cohen and Leon R. Kass — "Cast Me Not Off in Old Age," *Commentary*, January 2006.

Kurt Darr — "Assistance in Dying, Part II: Assisted Suicide in the United States," *Nexus*, Spring 2007.

Carol Davis	"Live and Let Go," *Nursing Standard*, October 26, 2005.
Elliot N. Dorff	"End-of-Life: Jewish Perspectives," *Lancet*, September 3, 2005.
H. Tristram Engelhardt Jr. and Ana Smith Iltis	"End-of-Life: The Traditional Christian View," *Lancet*, September 17, 2005.
Mary Ersek	"Assisted Suicide: Unraveling a Complex Issue," *Nursing*, April 2005.
Shirley Firth	"End-of-Life: A Hindu View," *Lancet*, August 20, 2005.
Mary A. Fischer	"To Live or to Die," *Reader's Digest*, May 2003.
Matthew Fleischer	"The Semantics of Aid in Dying," *LA Weekly*, April 18, 2007.
Kathleen M. Foley	"Is Physician-Assisted Suicide Ever Acceptable? It's Never Acceptable." *Family Practice News*, June 1, 2007.
Michael E. Gill	"A Moral Defense of Oregon's Assisted-Suicide Law," *Mortality*, February 2005.
Faye Girsh	"Ashcroft, Eastwood and Assisted Dying," *Humanist*, May/June 2005.
Nancy Harvey	"Dying Like a Dog," *Human Life Review*, Winter 2005.

Cindy Ellen Hill   "Death with Dignity: Invoking Compassion—and Caution—in the Debate," *Vermont Woman*, December 2007.

Susan Horsburgh,   "Her Son's Last Wish," *People*, October 13, 2003.
Dietlind Lerner,
and Bryce
Corbett

Garret Keizer   "Life Everlasting: The Religious Right and the Right to Die," *Harper's*, February 2005.

Damien Keown   "End-of-Life: The Buddhist View," *Lancet*, September 10, 2005.

Daniel E. Lee   "Physician-Assisted Suicide: A Conservative Critique of Intervention," *Hastings Center Report*, January-February 2003.

Rita L. Marker   "Patience and Plastic Bags," *Human Life Review*, Spring 2003.

Rita L. Marker   "Suicide by Any Other Name," *Human Life Review*, Winter 2007.

Hazel Markwell   "End-of-Life: A Catholic View," *Lancet*, September 24, 2005.

Diane Martindale   "A Culture of Death," *Scientific American*, June 2005.

Marc   "Death over the Counter," *National Catholic Reporter*, September 23, 2005.
Mazgon-
Fernandes

Michael J. McManus	"Oregon's Assisted Suicide," *Washington Times*, June 16, 2007.
Gilbert Meilaender	"Living Life's End," *First Things*, May 2005.
Robert D. Orr and Gilbert Meilaender	"Ethics and Life's Ending: An Exchange," *Current*, October 2004.
Michael Petrou	"A Time to Die," *Maclean's*, September 5, 2005.
Ramesh Ponnuru	"Reasons to Live: The Rational Case Against Euthanasia," *National Review*, April 25, 2005.
Timothy E. Quill	"Is Physician-Assisted Suicide Ever Acceptable? It's Justified in Rare Cases," *Family Practice News*, June 1, 2007.
Betty Rollin	"Path to a Peaceful Death," *Washington Post*, May 30, 2004.
Margot Roosevelt	"Choosing Their Time," *Time*, April 4, 2005.
Abdulaziz Sachedina	"End-of-Life: The Islamic View," *Lancet*, August 27, 2005.
Jeffrey A. Schaler	"Living and Dying the State"s Way, *Liberty*, August 2003.
Thomas Schirrmacher	"Medical Killing—an Evangelical Perspective," *Christian Bioethics*, August 2003.

Paul T.
Schotsmans

"The Ethical Claim of a Dying Brother," *Christian Bioethics*, August 2003.

Jeff Shannon

"Frankie, Maggie and Me: Inside the Million Dollar Maelstrom," *New Mobility*, April 2005.

Wesley J. Smith

"A Duty to Die?" *Human Life Review*, Winter 2004.

Wesley J. Smith

"Million Dollar Missed Opportunity: What Clint Eastwood's Oscar-Winning Movie Could Have Done," *Weekly Standard*, March 1, 2005.

Wesley J. Smith

"The Future of Assisted Suicide and Euthanasia," *First Things*, April 16, 2007.

Laura Spinney

"Last Rights," *New Scientist*, April 23, 2005.

Carl Wellman

"A Legal Right to Physician-Assisted Suicide Defended," *Social Theory and Practice*, January 2003.

Index

A

Abortion analogy, PAS, 42–43, 45, 60–61

Abuses/abuse potential, PAS
of economically disadvantaged, 58
from legalization, 65, 109, 139
of lethal drugs, 116
protection from, 41
universal healthcare, lack of, 46

Academy of Hospice and Palliative Care Medicine (AAHPM), 32

Accomplice liability, assisted suicide, 197

Acquired Immune Deficiency Syndrome (AIDS), 127, 130, 133–134

Admiraal, Pieter, 180

Advance Medical Directive, 76

Age-rationing, prolonging life, 85

Aid in dying, as terminology, 17, 31–33, 44, 77, 119–121, 147

AIDS. *See* Acquired Immune Deficiency Syndrome

Alzheimer's disease, 83, 133, 191

American College of Physicians, 131

American Geriatrics Society (AGS), 56–59

American Journal of Psychiatry (journal), 113

American Medical News (journal), 174

American Medical Women's Association (AMWA), 33

American Public Health Association (APHA), 33, 120–121, 124

Americans Disabled for Attendant Programs Today (ADAPT), 97

Appel, Jacob M., 110–111, 114

Arizona law, assisted suicide, 190

Arnold, Uwe-Christian, 38–43

Asch, Adrienne, 97–103

Ashcroft, John, 19, 144

Assisted suicide
accomplice liability, 197
Arizona law, 190
cancer patients, 92, 117, 133
depressed patients, 110
ethics of, 24–25, 126
low-income opposition to, 45–48
See also Physician-assisted death; Physician-assisted suicide; Suicide

At Death's Window (Lamott), 92

Australia, PAS, 140–141

Autonomy/self-determination
in Christian beliefs, 93
for disabled persons, 100
government interference, 27
individual, 114
informed consent, 74
legal right, PAS, 23
limits, 56, 59
loss of, 117, 119
moral right, 23, 27–28
Oregon PAS, law, 104–106
religious/spiritual principles, 74–75

B

Bagenstos, Samuel R., 60–63

Barrett, Cynthia, 170

218

Battin, Margaret Pabst, 79–90, 126–127, 130–134, 144

Becoming at Home in the World (Phifer), 70

Belgium, PAS, 138, 140–141

Bioethicists, duty to die, 66

Blevins, Dean, 154–162

Body *vs.* spirit, suffering, 69

Bouvia, Elizabeth, 98–99

Bowden, Thomas A., 35–37

Bridgman, Percy, 35–36

British Medical Association, 166

Brongersma, Edward, 165

Buchanan, Allen, 79

Burt, Robert, 99

Bush, George W., 144–145

C

California Medical Association (CMA), 31–34

Californians Against Assisted Suicide, 53–54

Callahan, Dan, 80, 85–87

Cancer patients, 31, 92, 117, 133

Casey, Donna, 163–167

Center for Ethics in Health Care (Oregon Health & Science University), 148

Central Arkansas Veterans Healthcare System, 154

Cheney, Kate, 171

Christian beliefs
    autonomy in, 93
    conservative doctrine, 32
    against euthanasia, 68–69
    influence of, 166
    morality of, 65, 94–96
    violation of, 91–96

Clinton, Bill, 144

CMA. *See* California Medical Association

Colburn, Don, 146–153

Compassion & Choices organization (C&C), 53, 118, 121–123, 149, 153

Compassion in Dying (citizens group), 97, 157

Controlled Substances Act (CSA), 19, 144

Countertransference, PAS, 187–188

D

Daniels, Norman, 79–80, 83–84

De Assis, Machado, 67

Death/dying
    dementia patients, 131, 171
    depressed patients, 172
    with dignity, 22, 25–27
    of disabled persons, 99–101
    freedom to choose, 151–152
    individual choice, 35–37
    medically hastened, 31–34
    medicine to prolong, 40
    on-demand, 111, 114
    open discussion, 148
    PAS complications, 115, 169–171
    patient fear, 58–59
    peaceful result, 146–148
    planned, 146–148
    request for by patient, 57
    right-to-death, implied, 36–37
    See also Oregon Death with Dignity Act; Oregon PAS; Physician-assisted death; Physician-assisted suicide; Suicide

Death with Dignity Law. *See* Oregon Death with Dignity Act

Declaration of Independence, rights, 36

DeFazio, Peter, 144

Dementia patients, PAS, 131, 171
Depression/depressed patients
  assisted suicide for, 110
  and PAD requests, 41, 155,
    159, 161
  patient deaths, 172
  right-to-die for, 155–156
  suicide, assisting illegally, 195
  treatment for, 159–160
  undiagnosed, 51
  See also Patients/patient con-
    trol; Terminally ill patients
Dignitas (Swiss right-to-die
  group), 38–39, 163–164, 199–201
Dignitate (German right-to-die
  group), 38
Disabled persons
  activism for, 60–63
  bias against assisted suicide,
    60
  coercion against, 62
  communication with, 100–101
  death of, 99–101
  health-care professional dis-
    comfort, 99–100
  legalization impact, 53–55,
    60–63
  patient autonomy, 100
  psychological/social needs, 98
  quality of life, 61, 98–99, 103
  right to die, 61, 66
  rights groups, 46, 50–52,
    97–98
  social issues, 62–63, 99–101
  treatment withdrawal, 98
Doctors. *See* Physicians
Double effect principle, PAS,
  77–78
DPA news agency, 199–201
Due Process clause, U.S. Constitution, 17–18
Duty to die
  bioethicists, 66

distributive issue, 80
global differences, life expectancy, 81–82
and health care, 79–90
health-care reorganization
  results, 79–90
life-prolonging medicine, 80
lifespan equity, 89
morality of, 79–90
rational self-interest, 83–84
religious traditions, 80
resource conservation, 88
varieties of, 79–80
Dworkin, Ronald, 24

E

Edwards, Miles, 100–101
Eighmey, George, 149, 151–153
Elderly Americans, slippery slope
  effect, 133–134
Emanuel, E.J., 180
End-of-life care, 31
Enouen, Susan W., 115–119
Equal Protection clause, U.S. Constitution, 18
Ethics
  of assisted suicide, 24–25, 126
  bioethicists, 66
  and euphemisms, 120
  morality of, 73–74
  physicians' code, 187
  of suffering, 74
  of VAE, 135–138
Ethics committees, role in PAS,
  41–42
Euphemisms, PAS acceptance,
  120–125
European support, of PAS, 163–
  166
Euthanasia
  Christian beliefs against,
    68–69

control of, 128
Holland law, 164–166
involuntary, 50, 119
legalization, 68, 115–119, 165
Nazi link, 39
nonvoluntary, 140
opponents of, 127
and sanctity-of-life, 69
slippery slope effect, 109, 115–119, 126
See also Voluntary Active Euthanasia
Euthanasia, PAS *vs.*, 108, 119
Euthanasia and the Law in the Netherlands (Griffiths, Bood, Weyers), 165
Euthanasia Prevention Coalition, 127
EXIT (Swiss right-to-die group), 41

F

Family involvement, PAS, 175
Fatal Freedom: The Ethics and Politics of Suicide (Szasz)
Favuzzi, Teresa, 53–55
Final Exit: The Practicalities of Self-Deliverance and Assisted Suicide for the Dying (Humphrey), 191
Final Exit Network, 190–192, 194–196
Fogarty, Colin, 143–145
Fourteenth Amendment, U. S. Constitution, 17–18
Free will, 67–69
Freedom to choose, 66, 136–138, 151–152
Freeland, Michael J., 113

G

Gabbard, Glen O., 187
Gerber, Urs, 200
Germany, right-to-die, 38–43
Gonzales v. Oregon, 17, 19
Goodwin, Peter, 104–105, 122
Gregson, Julie, 38–43
Griffiths, John, 165–166
Groningen Academic Hospital (Holland), 128
Groningen protocol, 165

H

Hale-Rowe, Wye, 190, 193–195
Hamilton, C.A., 185
Hamilton, George, 175
Hamilton, N.G., 185
Hardwig, John, 80–82
Harm-to-others, 32, 66, 135–141
HCD Research, physician-assisted suicide survey, 32
Health care/insurance
disabled persons, professional discomfort, 99–100
global, 81–82, 87
individual choice, 77
legalization risk, uninsured, 44–52
pain control, 178
resources, duty to die, 79–90
for terminally ill, 66
vulnerable people, 47
Health maintenance organization (HMO), 173–174
The Hemlock Society, 53, 94, 157, 196
See also Compassion & Choices
Hippocratic Oath, 68

Hold On: Getting Through Tough Times (Phifer), 70

Holland. *See* The Netherlands

Hospice
    care standards, 176–177
    Germany system, 40–41
    health care system reform, 77
    medical resource allocation, 28–29
    Oregon PAS, 117, 183
    PAS as alternative, 147
    quality of life, 98

Humphrey, Derek, 190–191

Huntington's disease, 83

Hypothetical scenarios, PAD study, 155–156

I

Ikeda, Richard, 31–34

Impaired judgment, 98, 105, 113, 144, 172

Infanticide, 119, 128, 165

Informed consent, autonomy, 74–75

International Task Force on Euthanasia and Assisted Suicide, 119

Intolerable suffering
    from mental causes, 23
    and pain, 28, 118–119, 132
    by right-holders, 22
    right to die, 27–29, 56
    social bias, 128
    See also Suffering

Involuntary euthanasia, 50, 119

J

Jalsevac, Meg, 126–129

Jefferson, Thomas, 67–68

Joffe, Joel, 166–167

John Paul II (Pope), 78

Jones, Robert P., 44–52

Jonquire, Rob, 47–48

Journal of Medical Ethics, 31, 126

Judeo-Christian legacy, PAS, 68–69

K

Kass, Leon, 184

Kelly, R., 187

Kevorkian, Jack
    Frederick, Merian, 70
    nonterminal patients, 112–113
    right-to-die, 60
    terminally ill patients, 69

L

Lamm, Richard, 79

Lamott, Anne, 91–96

Langsner, Frank, 190–194

Lee, Barbara, 143–144

Legal rights
    arguments against, 28–29
    autonomy/self-determination, 23, 27–28
    death with dignity, 22, 25–27
    individual death choice, 35–37
    morality, 24
    right-holders, 22–25
    suffering, relief efforts, 28–30
    unnecessary suffering, 22, 24–25

Legality/legalization
    abuses by, 65, 109, 139
    changes unlikely, 145
    Christian beliefs violation, 91–96
    controversy of, 143–145
    disabled, impact on, 53–55, 60–63
    euthanasia, 68, 115–119, 165
    expansion-of-care options thwarted, 59

freedom to choose, 136–138
infanticide, 119
legal rights of, 22–30, 35–37
life, devaluation of, 53–55
majority, favored by, 40–41
medically hastened deaths,
    31–34
patient trust, undermining,
    56–59
patient *vs.* physician empow-
    erment, 104–106
peaceful death result, 146–148
and physicians, 32–34, 104–
    106
precedent, Germany, 41
right-to-kill, 135–136
risk for uninsured, 44–52
slippery slope effect, 138–140
social needs of, 38–43
studies on, 140–141
suicide increase not found,
    130–134
uninsured, risks of, 44–52
of VAE, 56–59
vulnerable persons, 51, 131,
    135–141, 166
wish to die, 97–103
*Liberalism's Troubled Search for
Equality: Religion and Cultural
Bias in the Oregon Physician-
Assisted Suicide Debates* (Jones),
44
Liberty-rights package, 29
Life/lifespan
    expectancies, 82, 88–90
    extending, 86
    global differences, 81–82
    limited, 57
    meaning of, 65
    relative value, 71
    religious/spiritual respect for,
        72–73
Life-prolonging intervention, for-
    going, 58

Llosa, Alvaro Vargas, 67–69
Low-income opposition, to as-
    sisted suicide, 45–48

M

Manslaughter charges, 190–191
Marker, Rita L., 120–125, 168–178
Masci, David, 44–52
Matheny, Patrick, 169
Meaning of life, religious beliefs,
    65
Medicaid/Medicare program, Or-
    egon, 172
Medical Durable Power of Attor-
    ney, 76
Medically hastened death, 31–33,
    40, 116, 173
Mental illness/distress, 23, 112,
    191–193
Mill, John Stewart, 136–137
Miller, Paul, 62
Millet, Lisa, 177
Million Dollar Baby (movie), 97
Minelli, Ludwig, 163–164, 199–201
Mohler, Albert, 91–96
Morality/moral choices
    autonomy/self-determination,
        23, 27–28
    Christian beliefs, 65, 94–96
    duty to die, 79–90
    ethics, 73–74
    vs. free will, 67–69
    legal rights of, 24
    vs. legality, 65
    meaning of life, 65
    of pain, 73
    of physicians, 57
    religious/spiritual principles,
        65, 70–78, 73–74
Muralt, Hans, 201

N

Nazi Party, euthanasia link, 39
The Netherlands (Holland)
   complications, PAS, 115, 170–171
   emotional burden of PAS, 180
   euthanasia law, 164–166
   individual suicide, no increases in, 130–134
   infanticide, 128
   involuntary euthanasia, 119
   nonterminal patient PAS, 112
   PAS studies, 139–140
   physicians, negatively affected by PAS, 180–181
   slippery slope effect, 165
   VAE in, 132, 135, 138
New England Journal of Medicine (NEJM), 170
Nock, Albert J., 67–68
Nonterminal patients, 109–114
Nonvoluntary euthanasia, 140
Not Dead Yet (organization), 60, 97, 103
Nuland, Sherwin, 170–171

O

O'Dell, Jane, 153
Oregon Death with Dignity Act
   and AIDS patients, 133
   demographic patterns, 157
   persons who use the, 123
   psychological conditions, 155
   reports on, 168
Oregon Department of Human Services (DHS)
   assisted suicide statistics, 123, 168
   data reliability, 116, 123, 132
   research results, 127–128

Oregon Health & Science University (Center for Ethics in Health Care), 148
Oregon PAS, data unreliability
   choice *vs.* requirement, 177–178
   death complications, 169–171
   dementia patients, 171
   depressed patients, 172
   doctor-patient relationship, 173–174
   doctors, protection for, 175–176
   family involvement, lack of, 175
   financial requests, 172
   HMO efforts, 174–175
   Medicaid program, 172
   PAS reported deaths, 168–169
   prescriptions, previously prescribed, 173
   suicide rate climbs, 177
Oregon PAS, law
   accountability/safeguards, 115
   advocacy group involvement, 118
   AIDS patients, 130
   autonomy, 104–106
   changes unlikely, 145
   conservative religious opposition, 36–37
   controversy over, 16–17, 19, 143–145
   effectiveness of, 143–145
   individual death choice, 35
   lethal drugs, unused prescriptions, 115
   nonterminal patient, 113
   patient impact, 115–117
   patient judgment, 105–106
   peer-reviewed research, 31–32
   physicians, negative impact on, 182–183
   psychiatric evaluation, 117

reports on, 113, 186–187
social issues, 101–103
suicide increases not found,
130–134
terminology for PAS, 123

P

PAD. *See* Physician-assisted death
Pain/pain relief
for family member, 109
health insurance for, 178
impaired judgment, 105
intolerable suffering, 28, 118–
119, 132
management, 33, 58, 77–78,
176–177
medication of, 58
morality in, 73
PAD study, 154, 159
patient control of, 33
physical decline with, 92
slippery slope, 108
Palliative care/medicine, 40–41, 98,
165
PAS. *See* Physician-assisted suicide
Patients/patient control
beliefs of, 154–155
cancer, 31, 92, 117, 133
dementia, 131, 171
determination, 185
nonterminal, 110–114
of pain, 33
physician relationship, 58,
173–174
request for death, 57
suicide, illegal assistance, 193–
196
undermining trust, 56, 57
See also Depression/depressed
patients; Terminally ill patients
Phifer, Kenneth W., 70–78

The Philosophers' Brief (court
brief), 23–24
Physician-assisted death (PAD)
aid in dying, 17, 31–33, 44,
77, 119–121, 147
cancer patients, 133
demographics of, 154
PAS euphemism, 123
patient beliefs, 154–155
psychological conditions, 155
psychosocial concerns, 157,
159, 162
terminally ill patients, 161
See also Death/dying; Oregon
Death with Dignity Act; Oregon PAS; Physician-assisted
suicide; Voluntary Active
Euthanasia
Physician-assisted death (PAD),
physical/psychological study
demographics, 154–155, 157
depressed patients, 41, 155,
159, 161
hypothetical scenarios, 155–
156, 159
pain, 154, 159
quality-of-life *vs.* sanctity-of-
life, 160
recruitment procedures, 157
religious beliefs, 154–155, 158,
160–162
results of, 158–160
study purpose, 156–157
values, 160–162
Physician-assisted suicide (PAS),
16
abortion analogy, 42–43, 45,
60–61
abuse potential, 41, 46, 58,
139
and Christian beliefs, 91–96
complications with, 115, 169–
171
countertransference, 187–188

definition of, 56

in dementia, 171

double-effect principle, 77–78

euphemisms, 120–125

European support, 163–167

good faith in, 176

nonterminal patients, availability of, 109–114

refusal of request, 173–174

terminally ill patients, 110–114

See also Oregon Death with Dignity Act; Oregon PAS; Physician-assisted death; Voluntary Active Euthanasia

Physician-patient relationship, 58, 173–174

Physicians

countertransference, 187–188

data lack for, 186–187

emotional burden, 180

ethical code, 187

investigation questions, 179–180

and legalization, 32–34, 104–106

moral rights of, 57

not always healers, 77–78

patient determination, 185

reports by, 169

safety roles of, 33

Physicians for Compassionate Care, 145, 179

Preston, Thomas A., 154–162

Pro-life proponents, 137

The Psychiatrist (de Assis), 67

Psychology. *See* Physician-assisted death (PAD), physical/psychological study

Psychosocial concerns, of PAD, 157, 159, 162

Q

Quality of life

disabled persons and, 61, 98–99, 103

hospice, 98

vs. sanctity-of-life, 103, 159–160

undermining patient trust, 57

R

Rational suicide, 110–111

Rawls, John, 79

Reagan, Peter, 183–184

Rehnguist, William (Chief Justice), 17, 20

Religious beliefs/principles

autonomy/self-determination, 74–75

community, individual connection, 75–77

conservatism, political influence, 35–37

duty to die, 80

existence, not absolute value, 72

life/lifespan, 72–73

meaning of life, 65

moral choices in, 65, 70–78, 73–74

opposition, assisted suicide, 48–50

Oregon PAS opposition, 36–37

in PAD study, 154–155, 158, 160–162

right-to-kill, 135–136

vs. social issues, 44

suffering, 74, 160–162

support of PAS, 70–78

See also Christian beliefs

Remmelink Report, 139–140

Request for death, by patient, 57

Richardson, Robert, 174–175
Richman, Sheldon, 104–106
Right-holders, PAS, 22–25
Right-to-die
    advocates, 144, 196
    autonomy, 74
    for depressed patients, 155–156
    Dignitas, 38–39, 163–164
    by disabled persons, 61, 66
    in Germany, 38–43
    and intolerable suffering, 27–29, 56
    issues, 135
    opposition to, 60
    organizations, 156
    terminal illness, 97, 110–114
    U.S. Constitution, 17–18
    See also Suicide
Right-to-kill, PAS legalization, 135–136
Right-to-life, 36–37, 60–61, 135
Roe v. Wade, 91
Roman Catholic Church, 137
Rubin, Paul, 189–198

S

Safeguards, medically hastened death, 33
San Jose Mercury News (newspaper), 53
Sanctity-of-life, 69, 103, 159–160
Satcher, David, 124
Schadenberg, Alex, 127–128
Schafer, Arthur, 164
Schiavo, Terri, 60, 137
Setting Limits (Callahan), 80
Slippery slope effect
    AIDS victims, 127, 133–134
    and CMA, 32
    data tracking, 131–132
    in elderly Americans, 133–134
    euthanasia concerns, 109, 115–119, 126
    evidence, 132–134
    in Holland, 165
    and legalization, 138–140
    nonterminal patients, 109
    pain relief, 108
    research validity, 126–129
    statistics on, 108
    suffering, 109
    vulnerable people, 31, 126–127, 130
Smith, Wesley J., 110–114, 119, 120–125
Social issues/needs
    bias with, 128
    disabled persons, 62–63, 99–101
    duty to die, 89
    intolerable suffering, 128
    legalization of assisted suicide, 38–43
    in Oregon PAS, 101–103
    progressive thinking, 164
    vs. psychosocial concerns, 157, 159, 162
    vs. religious conservatives, 44
    wish to die, 97–103
Stevens, Kenneth R., Jr., 145, 179–188
Suffering
    body *vs.* spirit, 69
    ethics of, 74
    of family member, 109
    infanticide, 165
    with mental disorder, 112
    relief efforts, 28–30
    religious/spiritual principles, 74, 160–162
    slippery slope effect, 109
    unbearable, 165

unnecessary, 22, 24–25
See also Intolerable suffering
Suicide
accomplice liability, 197
Arizona law, 190
depression, 161, 195
euphemisms for, 119, 122
as experienced guides, 196–198
individual *vs.* assisted, 66
legalization doesn't cause increases in, 130–134
manslaughter, 190–191
mental illness, 191–193
neighborhoods object, 200–201
Oregon rate climbs, 177
patient relationships with, 193–196
pressure to choose, 54–55
in public places, 199–201
rational for, 110–111
Switzerland, 199–201
See also Death/dying; Oregon Death with Dignity Act; Oregon PAS; Physician-assisted death; Physician-assisted suicide; Right-to-die
A Suicide Right for the Mentally Ill? (Appel), 110–111
Svart, Lovelle, 146–153
Switzerland, 112, 138, 163–164
Szasz, Thomas, 106

T

Taking Care of Strangers (Burt), 99–100
Terminally ill patients
demographic concerns, 144
health care for, 66
hypothetical scenarios, 156
and PAD, 161
PAS not restricted to, 110–114

on respirators, 141
right to die, 97
See also Depression/depressed patients; Patients/patient control
Terminology
aid in dying, 17, 31–33, 44, 77, 119–121, 147
for PAS advocates, 124–125
PAS misnamed, 106
Thomas, Vicki, 194
Tolle, Susan, 100–101, 148
Tucker, Kathryn, 123

U

Unbearable suffering, 165
Uninsured Americans, 45–46, 133–134
United Kingdom (U.K.), 166–167
United States Constitution, 17–18
United States Supreme Court, 17, 145
University of Utah, 130–134
Unnecessary suffering, 22, 24–25

V

Vacco v. Quill, 17–19
VAE. *See* Voluntary Active Euthanasia
Varghese, F.T., 187
Vermont, PAS legislation, 120
Voluntary Active Euthanasia (VAE)
ethics of, 135–138
legalization of, 56–59
in the Netherlands, 132
opponents of, 139
See also Euthanasia; Physician-assisted death; Physician-assisted suicide
Voorhies, Jana, 189–198

Vulnerable people
  current health care, 47
  legalization of PAS, 51, 131,
    135–141, 166
  slippery slope effect, 31, 126–
    127, 130
  uninsured, 46

W

Washington v. Glucksberg, 17, 99
Wellman, Carl, 22–30
Werth, James L, Jr., 154–162
Wish to die, as social/medical is-
  sue, 97–103